Tiffany and the Lowlifes

Ian Wolf

Pacific Area Communications

For information address:
Pacific Area Communications
PO Box 1045
Ione, CA 95640

Telephone orders:
(209) 274-6700 or fax (209) 274-6767

Printed in the United States of America

Chapter 1

There was once a little rich girl whose father was a powerful man who owned a great company full of buildings and money. His home was built upon one of the hills of San Francisco, and was very grand and beautiful. The little girl, whose name was Tiffany, was born there, but she was sent soon after her birth, because her mother was not very strong, to be brought up by people who worked for her father. They lived in a large house on the side of another hill in San Francisco, about halfway toward the Bay.

The little rich girl was a sweet little creature, and at the time my story begins was about eight years old, but she got older very fast. Her face was fair and pretty, with eyes like two bits of night sky, each with a star dissolved in the blue. Those eyes you would have thought must have known they came from there, so often were they turned up in that direction. The ceiling of her nursery was blue, with stars in it, as much like the sky as they could make it. But I doubt if ever she saw the real sky with the stars in it, for a reason, which I had better mention at once.

These big cities were full of dark places underneath; huge parking garages, and winding ways, some with water running through them, and some shining with all colors of the rainbow when a light was taken in. There would not have been much known about them, had there not been telephone and electric lines in them. In the course of repair work, the phone men and PG&E workers came upon many of these strange places. A few of them had far-off openings out on the side of the ocean, or into the bay.

Now in these subterranean caverns, and even in some of the darker streets above, lived a strange race of beings, called by some bums, by some tramps, by some lowlifes. There was a legend current in the country that at one time they lived normal lives, and were very like other people. But for some reason or other, concerning which there were different legendary theories, the governor had laid what they thought too severe taxes upon them, or had required observances of them they did not like, or had begun to treat them with more severity, in some way or other, and impose stricter laws; the consequence was that they had all disappeared from the face of the country during daylight. According to the legend, however, instead of going to some other country or city, they had all taken refuge in the subterranean caverns, from whence they never came out but at night, and then seldom showed themselves in any numbers, and never to many people at once. It was only in the least frequented and most difficult parts of the city that they were said to gather even at night in the open air. Those who had caught sight of any of them said that they had greatly altered in the course of generations; and no wonder, seeing they lived away from the sun, in cold and wet and dark places. They were now, not ordinarily ugly, but either absolutely hideous, or ludicrously grotesque both in face and form. There was no invention, they said, of the most lawless imagination expressed by pen or pencil that could surpass the extravagance of their appearance. But I suspect those who said so had mistaken some of their animal companions for the lowlifes themselves...of which more by and by. The lowlifes themselves were not so far removed from the human, as such a description would imply. And as they grew misshapen in body they had grown in knowledge and cleverness, and now were able to do things no normal person could see the possibility of. But as they grew in cunning, they grew in mischief, and their great delight was in every way they could think of to annoy the people who lived in the open-air world above them. They had enough affection left for each other to preserve them from being absolutely cruel for cruelty's sake to those that came in their way; but still they so heartily cherished the ancestral grudge against those who occupied their former possessions, and especially against the descendants of the company owner who had caused many of them to lose their jobs, that they sought every opportunity of tormenting normal people in ways that were as odd as their inventors; and although sickly and misshapen, they had strength equal to their cunning. In the process of time they had gotten a leader and a type of government of their own, whose chief business, beyond their own simple affairs, was to devise trouble for their neighbors. It will now be pretty evident why the little rich girl had never seen the sky at night. They were much too afraid of the lowlifes to let her out of the house then, even in company with ever so many attendants; and they had good reason, as we shall see by and by.

Chapter 2

I have said that the little rich girl Tiffany was about eight years old when my story begins. And this is how it begins.

One very wet day, when the city was covered with mist, which was constantly gathering itself together into raindrops, and pouring down on the roofs of the great old house, whence it fell in a fringe of water from the eaves all round about it, Tiffany could not of course go out. She got very tired, so tired that even her toys could no longer amuse her. You would wonder at that if I had time to describe to you one half of the toys she had. But then, you wouldn't have the toys themselves, and that makes all the difference: you can't get tired of a thing before you have it. It was a picture, though, worth seeing... the rich girl sitting in the nursery with the sky ceiling over her head, as a great table covered with her toys. If the artist would like to draw this, I should advise them not to meddle with the toys. I am afraid of attempting to describe them, and I think an artist had better not try to draw them. They can do a thousand things I can't, but I don't think they could draw those toys. Nobody could better make the little rich girl herself than a fine artist could, though... leaning with her back bowed into the back of the chair, her head hanging down, arid her hands in her lap, very miserable as she would say herself, not even knowing what she would like, except it were to go out and get thoroughly wet, and catch a particularly nice cold, and have to go to bed and take medicine. The next moment after you see her sitting there, her nurse goes out of the room.

Even that is a change, and Tiffany wakes up a little, and looks about her. Then she tumbles off her chair, and runs out the door, not the same door the nurse went out of, but one that opened at the foot of a curious old stair of painted oak, which looked as if never anyone had set foot upon it. She had once before been up six steps, and that was sufficient reason, in such a day, for trying to find out what was at the top of it.

Up and up she ran... such a long way it seemed to her! Until she came to the top of the third flight. There she found the landing was the end of a long passage. Into this she ran. It was full of doors on each side. There were so many that she did not care to open any, but ran on to the end, where she turned into another passage, also full of doors. When she had turned twice more, and still saw doors and only doors about her, she began to get frightened. It was so silent! And all those doors must hide rooms with nobody in them! That was dreadful. Also the rain made a great trampling noise on the roof. She turned and started at full speed, her little footsteps echoing through the sounds of the rain...back for the stairs and her safe nursery. So she thought, but she had lost herself long ago. It doesn't follow that she was lost, because she had lost herself, though.

She ran for some distance, turned several times, and then began to be afraid. Very soon she was sure that she had lost the way back. Rooms everywhere, and no stair! Her little heart beat as fast as her little feet ran, and a lump of tears was growing in her throat. But she was too eager and perhaps too frightened to cry for some time. At last her hope failed her. Nothing but passages and doors everywhere! She threw herself on the floor, and burst into a wailing cry broken by sobs.

She did not cry long, however, for she was as brave as could be expected of a little girl her age. After a good cry, she got up, and brushed the dust from her frock. Oh, what old dust it was! Then she wiped her eyes with her hands, for little rich girls don't always have their handkerchiefs in their pockets, any more than some other little girls I know of. Next, like a true young lady, she resolved on going wisely to work to find her way back: she would walk through the passages, and look in every direction for the stair. This she did, but without success. She went over the same ground again and again without knowing it, for the passages and doors were all alike. At last, in a corner, through a half-open door, she did see a stair. But alas! It went the wrong way: instead of going down, it went up. Frightened as she was, however, she could not help wishing to see where yet further the stair could lead. It was very narrow, and so steep that she went on like a four-legged creature on her hands and feet.

Chapter 3

Whe came to the top, she found herself in a little square place, with three doors, two opposite each other, and one opposite the top of the stair. She stood for a moment, without an idea in her little head what to do next. But as she stood, she began to hear a curious humming sound. Could it be the rain? No. It was much gentler and even more monotonous than the sound of the rain, which now she scarcely heard. The low sweet humming sound went on, sometimes stopping for a little while and then beginning again. It was more like the hum of a very happy bee that had found a rich well of honey in some globular flower, than anything else I can think of at this moment. Where could it come from? She laid her ear first to one of the doors to hearken if it was there...then to another. When she laid her ear against the third door, there could be no doubt where it came from; it must be from something in that room. What could it be? She was rather afraid, but her curiosity was stronger than her fear, and she opened the door very gently and peeped in. What do you think she saw? A very old lady who sat watching a television with no sound.

Perhaps you will wonder how Tiffany could tell that the old lady was an old lady, when I inform you that not only was she beautiful, but her skin was smooth and white. I will tell you more. Her hair was combed back from her forehead and face and hung loose far down and all over her back. That is not much like an old lady... is it? Ah! But it was white almost as snow. And although her face was so smooth, her eyes looked so wise that you could not have helped seeing she must be old. Tiffany, though she could not have told you why, did think her very old indeed... quite sixty, she said to herself. But she was rather older than that, as you shall hear.

While Tiffany stared bewildered, with her head just inside the door, the old lady lifted hers, and said, in a sweet, but old and rather shaky voice, which mingled very pleasantly with the continued hum from her television: "Come in, my dear; come in. I am glad to see you."

That the little rich girl was a real rich girl you might see now quite plainly; for she didn't hang on to the handle of the door, and stare without moving, as I have known some do who ought to have been well brought up but were only rather vulgar little girls. She did as she was told, stepped inside the door at once, and shut it gently behind her.

"Come to me, my dear," said the old lady.

And again the little rich girl did as she was told. She approached the old lady...rather slowly, I confess, but did not stop until she stood by her side, and looked up in her face with her blue eyes and the two melted stars in them.

"Why, what have you been doing with your eyes, child?" asked the old lady.

"Crying," answered the little rich girl.

"Why, child?"

"Because I couldn't find my way down again."

"But you could find your way up."

"Not at first...not for a long time."

"But your face is streaked like the back of a zebra. Hadn't you a handkerchief to wipe your eyes with?"

"No."

"Then why didn't you come to me to wipe them for you?"

"Please, I didn't know you were here. I will next time."

"There's a good child!" said the old lady.

Then she turned off her television, rose, and going out of the room, returned with a little silver basin and a soft white towel, with which she washed and wiped the bright little face. And Tiffany thought her hands were so smooth and nice!

When she carried away the basin and towel, the little rich girl wondered to see how straight and tall she was, for, although she was so old, she didn't stoop a bit. She was dressed in black velvet with thick white heavy-looking lace about it, and on the black dress her hair shone like silver. There was hardly any more furniture in the room than there might have been in that of the poorest old woman who made her bread money by searching for sellable garbage. There was no carpet on the floor...no table anywhere... nothing but the television and the chair in front of it. When she came back, she sat down again, and without a word turned on the television once more, while Tiffany, who had never seen a television quite like this one, stood by her side and looked on. When the old lady had got herself deep into the next program, she said to the little rich girl, but without looking at her:

"Do you know my name, child?"

"No, I don't know it," answered the little rich girl.

"My name is Tiffany."

"That's my name!" cried the little rich girl.

"I know that. I let you have mine. I haven't got your name. You've got mine."

"How can that be?" asked the little rich girl, bewildered. "I've always had my name."

"Your papa, the big business man, asked me if I had any objection to your having it; and, of course, I hadn't. I let you have it with pleasure."

"It was very kind of you to give me your name... and such a pretty one," said the little rich girl.

"Oh, not so very kind!" said the old lady. "A name is one of those things one can give away and keep all the same. I have a good many such things. Wouldn't you like to know who I am child?"

"Yes, that I should...very much."

"I'm your great-great-grandmother," said the lady.

"What's that?" asked the little rich girl.

"I'm your father's mother's father's mother."

"Oh, dear! I can't understand that," said the little rich girl.

"I dare say not. I didn't expect you would. But that's no reason why I shouldn't say it."

"Oh, no!" answered the little rich girl.

"I will explain it all to you when you are older," the lady went on. "But you will be able to understand this much now: I came to take care of you."

"Is it long since you came? Was it yesterday? Or was it today, because it was so wet that I couldn't get out?"

"I've been here ever since you came yourself."

"What a long time!" said the little rich girl. "I don't remember it at all."

"No. I suppose not."

"But I never saw you before."

"No. But you shall see me again."

"Do you live in this room always?"

"I don't sleep in it. I sleep on the opposite side of the landing. I sit here most of the day."

"I shouldn't like it. My nursery is much prettier. You must be a rich lady too, if you are my great big grandmother."

"Yes, I am very rich."

"Where is your fine furniture and money, then?"

"In my bedroom."

"I should like to see them."

"You shall some day...not today."

"I wonder why nursie never told me."

"Nursie doesn't know. She never saw me."

"But somebody knows that you are in the house?"

"No; nobody."

"How do you get your dinner, then?"

"I keep poultry...of a sort."

"Where do you keep them?"

"I will show you."

"And who makes the chicken broth for you?"

"I never kill any of my chickens."

"Then I can't understand."

"What did you have for breakfast this morning?" asked the lady.

"Oh! I had bread and milk, and an egg...I bet you eat their eggs."

"Yes, that's it. I eat their eggs."

"Is that what makes your hair so white?"

"No, my dear. It's old age. I am very old."

"I thought so. Are you sixty?"

"Yes...more than that."

"Are you a hundred?"

"Yes...more than that. I am too old for you to guess. Come and see my chickens."

Again she stopped watching her television. She rose, took the little rich girl by the hand, led her out of the room, and opened the door opposite the stair. The little rich girl expected to see a lot of hens and chickens, but instead of that, she saw the blue sky first, and then the roofs of the house, with a multitude of the loveliest pigeons, mostly white, but of all colours, walking about, making bows to each other, and talking a language she could not understand. She clapped her hands with delight, and up rose such a flapping of wings that she in her turn was startled.

"You've frightened my poultry," said the old lady, smiling.

"And they've frightened me," said the little rich girl, smiling too. "But what very nice poultry! Are the eggs nice?"

"Yes, very nice."

"What a small egg-spoon you must have! Wouldn't it be better to keep hens, and get bigger eggs?"

"How should I feed them, though?"

"I see," said the rich girl. "The pigeons feed themselves. They've got wings."

"Just so. If they couldn't fly, I couldn't eat their eggs."

"But how do you get at the eggs? Where are their nests?"

The lady took hold of a little loop of string in the wall at the side of the door and, lifting a shutter, showed a great many pigeon-holes with nests, some with young ones and some with eggs in them. The birds came in at the other side, and she took out the eggs on this side. She closed it again quickly, lest the young ones should be frightened.

"Oh, what a nice way!" cried the little rich girl. "Will you give me an egg to eat? I'm rather hungry."

"I will some day, but now you must go back, or nursie will be miserable about you. I dare say she's looking for you everywhere."

"Except here," answered the little rich girl. "Oh, how surprised she will be when I tell her about my great big grand-grandmother!"

"Yes, that she will!" said the old lady with a curious smile. "Mind you tell her all about it exactly."

"That I will. Please will you take me back to her?"

"I can't go all the way, but I will take you to the top of the stair, and then you must run down quite fast into your own room."

The little rich girl put her hand in the old lady's, who, looking this way and that, brought her to the top of the first stair, and thence to the bottom of the second, and did not leave her till she saw her half-way down the third. When she heard the cry of her nurse's pleasure at finding her, she turned and walked up the stairs again, very fast indeed for such a very great grandmother, and sat down to her watching television with another strange smile on her sweet old face.

About this television of hers I will tell you more another time.

Guess what she was watching.

Chapter 4

"Why, where have you been, Tiffany?" asked the nurse, taking her in her arms. "It's very unkind of you to hide away so long. I began to be afraid..."

Here she checked herself.

"What were you afraid of, Nursie?" asked the little rich girl.

"Never mind," she answered. "Perhaps I will tell you another day. Now tell me where you have been."

"I've been up a long way to see my very great, huge, old grandmother," said the little rich girl.

"What do you mean by that?" asked the nurse, who thought she was making fun.

"I mean that I've been a long way up and up to see my GREAT grandmother. Ah, Nursie, you don't know what a beautiful mother of grandmothers I've got upstairs. She is such an old lady! With such lovely white hair...as white as my silver cup. Now, when I think of it, I thick her hair must be silver."

"What nonsense you are talking, Tiffany!" said the nurse.

"I'm not talking nonsense," returned Tiffany, rather offended. "I will tell you all about her. She's much taller than you are, and much prettier."

"Oh, I dare say!" remarked the nurse.

"And she lives upon pigeons' eggs."

"Most likely," said the nurse.

"And she sits in an empty room, watching television all day long."

"Not a doubt of it," said the nurse.

"And she keeps her fine furniture and money in her bedroom."

"Of course...quite the proper place to keep her money in. She counts it in bed, I'll bet."

"She didn't say that. And I don't think she does. I don't think my papa counts his money in bed. Does he, Nursie?"

"I never asked him. I dare say he does."

"And she's been there ever since I came here...ever so many years."

"Anybody could have told you that," said the nurse, who did not believe a word Tiffany was saying.

"Why didn't you tell me, then?"

"There was no necessity. You could make it all up for yourself."

"You don't believe me, then!" exclaimed the little rich girl, astonished and angry, as she well might be.

"Did you expect me to believe you, Tiffany?" asked the nurse coldly. "I know little rich girls are in the habit of telling make-believes, but you are the first I ever heard of who expected to have them believed," she added, seeing that the child was strangely in earnest.

The little rich girl burst into tears.

"Well, I must say," remarked the nurse, now thoroughly vexed with her for crying, "it is not at all becoming in a young lady to tell stories and expect to be believed just because she is rich."

"But it's quite true, I tell you."

"You've dreamt it, then, child."

"No, I didn't dream it. I went upstairs, and I lost myself, and if I hadn't found the beautiful lady, I should never have found myself."

"Oh, I dare say!"

"Well, you just come up with me, and see if I'm not telling the truth."

"Indeed I have other work to do. It's your dinner-time, and I won't have any more such nonsense."

14

The little rich girl wiped her eyes, and her face grew so hot that they were soon quite dry. She sat down to her dinner, but ate next to nothing. Not to be believed does not at all agree with little rich girls: for a real lady cannot tell a lie. So all the afternoon she did not speak a word. Only when the nurse spoke to her, she answered her, for a real lady is never rude...even when she does well to be offended.

Of course the nurse was not comfortable in her mind...not that she suspected the least truth in Tiffany's story, but that she loved her dearly, and was vexed with herself for having been so cross to her. She thought her crossness was the cause of the little rich girl's unhappiness, and had no idea that she was really and deeply hurt at not being believed. But, as it became more and more plain during the evening in her every motion and look that, although she tried to amuse herself with her toys, her heart was too confused and troubled to enjoy them, her nurse's discomfort grew and grew. When bedtime came, she undressed and laid her down, but the child, instead of holding up her little mouth to be kissed, turned away from her and lay still. Then Nursie's heart gave way altogether, and she began to cry. At the sound of her first sob the little rich girl turned again, and held her face to kiss her as usual. But the nurse had her handkerchief to her eyes, and did not see the movement.

"Nursie," said the princess, "why won't you believe me?"

"Because I can't believe you," said the nurse, getting angry again.

"Ah! Then, you can't help it," said Tiffany, "and I will not be mad with you any more. I will give you a kiss and go to sleep."

"You little angel!" cried the nurse, and caught her out of bed, and walked about the room with her in her arms, kissing and hugging her.

"You will let me take you to see my dear old great big grandmother, won't you?" said the little rich girl, as she laid her down again.

"And you won't say I'm ugly, any more. Will you, my dear?"

"Nursie, I never said you were ugly. What can you mean?"

"Well, if you didn't say it, you meant it."

"Indeed, I never did."

"You said I wasn't so pretty as that..."

"As my beautiful grandmother...yes, I did say that; and say it again, for it's quite true."

"Then I do think you are unkind!" said the nurse, and put her handkerchief to her eyes again.

"Nursie, dear, everybody can't be as beautiful as every other body, you know. You are very nice-looking, but if you had been as beautiful as my grandmother..."

"Bother your grandmother!" said the nurse.

"Nurse, that's very rude. You are not fit to be spoken to...till you can behave better."

The little rich girl turned away once more, and again the nurse was ashamed of herself.

"I'm sure I beg your pardon, Tiffany," she said, though still in an offended tone. But the little rich girl let the tone pass, and heeded only the words.

"You won't say it again, I am sure," she answered, once more turning towards her nurse. "I was only going to say that if you had been twice as nice-looking as you are, some rich man or other would have married you, and then what would have become of me?"

"You are an angel!" repeated the nurse, again embracing her.

"Now," insisted Tiffany, "you will come and see my grandmother...won't you?"

"I will go with you anywhere you like, my cherub," she answered; and in two minutes the weary little rich girl was fast asleep.

Chapter 5

When she woke the next morning, the first thing she heard was the rain still falling. Indeed, this day was so like the last that it would have been difficult to tell where was the use of it. The first thing she thought of, however, was not the rain, but the lady in the floors above; and the first question that occupied her thoughts was whether she should not ask the nurse to fulfill her promise this very morning, and go with her to find her grandmother as soon as she had had her breakfast. But she came to the conclusion that perhaps the lady would not be pleased if she took anyone to see her without first asking leave; especially as it was pretty evident, seeing she lived on pigeons' eggs, and cooked them herself, that she did not want the household to know she was there. So the little rich girl resolved to take the first opportunity of running up alone and asking whether she might bring her nurse. She believed the fact that she could not otherwise convince her she was telling the truth would have much weight with her grandmother.

The little rich girl and her nurse were the best of friends all dressing-time and Tiffany in consequence ate an enormous little breakfast.

"I wonder, Nursie"...that was her pet name for her nurse... "what pigeons' eggs taste like?" she said, as she was eating her egg...not quite a common one, for they always picked out the pinky ones for her.

"We'll get you a pigeon's egg, and you shall judge for yourself," said the nurse.

"Oh, no, no!" returned Tiffany, suddenly reflecting they might disturb the old lady in getting it, and that even if they did not, she would have one less in consequence.

"What a strange creature you are," said the nurse. "First to want a thing and then to refuse it!"

But she did not say it crossly, and the little rich girl never minded any remarks that were not unfriendly.

"Well, you see, Nursie, there are reasons," she returned, and said no more, for she did not want to bring up the subject of their former strife, lest her nurse should offer to go before she had had her grandmother's permission to bring her. Of course she could refuse to take her, but then she would believe her less than ever.

Now the nurse, as she said herself afterwards, could not be every moment in the room, and as never before yesterday had the little rich girl given her the smallest reason for anxiety, it had not yet come into her head to watch her more closely. So she soon gave her a chance, and the very first that offered, Tiffany was off and up the stairs again.

This day's adventure, however, did not turn out like yesterday's, although it began like it; and indeed today is very seldom like yesterday, if people would note the differences, even when it rains. The little rich girl ran through passage after passage, and could not find the stair of the floor above. My own suspicion is that she had not gone up high enough, and was searching on the second instead of the third floor. When she turned to go back, she failed equally in her search after the stair. She was lost once more.

Something made it even worse to bear this time, and it was no wonder that she cried again. Suddenly it occurred to her that it was after having cried before that she had found her grandmother's stair. She got up at once, wiped her eyes, and started upon a fresh quest. This time, although she did not find what she hoped, she found what was next best: she did not come on a stair that went up, but she came upon one that went down. It was evidently not the stair she had come up, yet it was a good deal better than none; so down she went, and was singing merrily before she reached the bottom. There, to her surprise, she found herself in the kitchen. Although she was not allowed to go there alone, her nurse had often taken her, and she was a great favourite with the servants. So there was a general rush at her the moment she appeared, for every one wanted to have her; and the report of where she was soon reached the nurse's ears. She came at once to fetch her; but she never suspected how she had got there, and the little rich girl kept her secret.

Her failure to find the old lady not only disappointed her, but made her very thoughtful. Sometimes she came almost to the nurse's opinion that she had dreamed all about her, but that idea never lasted very long. She wondered much whether she should ever see her again, and thought it very sad not to have been able to find her when she particularly wanted her. She resolved to say nothing more to her nurse on the subject, seeing it was so little in her power to prove her words.

Chapter 6

The next day the great cloud still hung over the skyscrapers, and the rain poured like water from a full sponge. The little rich girl was very fond of being out of doors, and she nearly cried when she saw that the weather was no better. But the mist was not of such a dark dingy grey; there was light in it; and as the hours went on it grew brighter and brighter, until it was almost too brilliant to look at; and late in the afternoon the sun broke out so gloriously that Tiffany clapped her hands, crying:

"See, see, Nursie! The sun has had his face washed. Look how bright he is! Do get my hat, and let us go out for a walk. Oh, dear! Oh dear! How happy I am!"

The nurse was very glad to please the little rich girl. She got her hat and cloak, and they set out together for a walk up the hill; for the road was so hard and steep that the water could not rest upon it, and it was always dry enough for walking a few minutes after the rain ceased. The clouds were rolling away in broken pieces, like great, overwoolly sheep, whose wool the sun had bleached till it was almost too white for the eyes to bear. Between them the sky shone with a deeper and purer blue, because of the rain. The trees on the roadside were hung all over with drops, which sparkled in the sun like jewels. The only things that were no brighter for the rain were the buses that ran down the roadways; they had changed from dirty black to muddy brown; but what they lost in colour they gained in sound...or at least in noise, for a bus when it charges through the big puddles after a rain storm makes wonderful vocalizations on the condition of the roads. But Tiffany was in raptures with the great brown buses rumbling down everywhere; and Nursie shared in her delight, for she too had been confined to the house for three days. At length she observed that the sun was getting low, and said it was time to be going back. She made the remark again and again, but every time, the little rich girl begged her to go on just a little farther and a little farther; reminding her that it was much easier to go downhill, and saying that when they did turn they would be at home in a moment. So on and on they did go, now to look at a group of ferns in one of the parks, now to pick a shining penny from a gutter, now to watch the flight of some bird. Suddenly the shadow of a great building top came up from behind, and shot in front of them. When the nurse saw it, she started and shook, and catching hold of the little rich girl's hand, turned and began to run down the hill.

"What's the problem, Nursie?" asked Tiffany, running alongside of her.

"We must not be out a moment longer."

"But we can't help being out a good many moments longer."

It was too true. The nurse almost cried. They were much too far from home. It was against express orders to be out with the little rich girl one moment after the sun was down; and they were nearly a mile up and over the hilltop and too close to the wrong part of the city! If Tiffany's father were to hear of it, Nursie would certainly be dismissed; and to leave the little rich girl would break her heart. It was no wonder she ran. But Tiffany was not in the least frightened, not knowing anything to be frightened at. She kept on chattering as well as she could, but it was not easy.

"Nursie! Nursie! Why do you run so fast? It shakes my teeth when I talk."

"Then don't talk," said Nursie.

But the little rich girl went on talking. She was always saying, "Look, look, Nursie!" but Nursie paid no more heed to anything she said, only ran on.

"Look, look, Nursie! Don't you see that funny man peeping over the garbage cans?"

Nursie only ran the faster. They had to pass the garbage cans, and when they came nearer, the little rich girl saw it was only a lump of garbage itself that she had taken for a man.

"Look, look, Nursie! There's such a curious creature at the foot of that old tree. Look at it, Nursie! It's making faces at us, I think!"

Nursie gave a stifled cry, something about where were the buses or police when you needed them, and ran faster still...so fast that Tiffany's little legs could not keep up with her, and she fell with a crash. It was a hard downhill road, and she had been running very fast...so it was no wonder she began to cry. This put the nurse nearly beside herself; but all she could do was to run on, the moment she got the little rich girl on her feet again.

"Who's that laughing at me?" said the little rich girl, trying to keep in her sobs, and running too fast for her grazed knees.

"Nobody, child," said the nurse, almost angrily.

But that instant there came a burst of coarse tittering from somewhere near, and a hoarse indistinct voice that seemed to say: "Lies! lies! lies!"

"Oh!" cried the nurse with a sigh that was almost a scream, and ran on faster than ever.

"Nursie! Nursie! I can't run any more. Do let us walk a bit."

"What I am to do?" said the nurse. "Here, I will carry you."

She caught her up; but found her much too heavy to run with, and had to set her down again. Then she looked wildly about her, gave a great cry, and said:

"We've taken the wrong turn somewhere, and I don't know this part of the city. We are lost, lost!"

The terror she was in had quite bewildered her. It was true enough they had lost the way. They had been running down into a little valley in which there were nothing but old half-ruined houses to be seen.

Tiffany and the Lowlifes

Now Tiffany did not know what good reason there was for her nurse's terror, for the servants all had strict orders never to mention the poor people or lowlifes to her, but it was very discomposing to see her nurse in such a fright. However, before she had time to grow thoroughly alarmed like her, she heard the sound of voices, and that revived her. Presently she saw a boy coming up the road from the valley to meet them. He was the singer; but before they met his song changed. And this is something like what he sang:

"Smash! Crash! Bang!
I'm as bad as a gang!
The boy ain't no bore!
Hiss and puff and roar!
If ya want to throw rocks!
I'll shave off your locks...
See the shining money!
One, two, three...
Bright as gold can be!
Four, five, six...
I'll beat ya off with sticks!
Seven, eight, nine...
What's mine is mine.
Ten, eleven, twelve...
I'll hit you with a helve.
We're the merry Mission-boys,
Make the lowlifes hold their noise."

"I wish you would hold your noise," said the nurse rudely, for the very word lowlife at such a time and in such a place made her tremble. It would bring the lowlifes upon them to a certainty, she thought, to defy them in that way. But whether the boy heard her or not, he did not stop his singing.

"Thirteen, fourteen, fifteen...
My pockets ain't worth siftin';
Sixteen, seventeen, eighteen...
That's the prettiest girl I ever seen.

Nineteen, twenty…

Lowlifes a plenty."

"Do be quiet," cried the nurse in a whispered shriek. But the boy, who was now close at hand, still went on.

"Hush! Run! Scurry!

There you go in a hurry!"

"There!" said the boy, as he stood still opposite them. "There! That'll do for them. They can't bear singing, and they can't stand that rap. They can't sing or rap themselves, for they ain't got no more voice than a sea gull under a taxi tire; and they don't like other people to sing."

The boy was dressed in a basketball jacket, with a curious cap on his head. He was a very nice-looking boy, with eyes as dark as the tar on the streets where he played and as sparkling as the street lights above. He was about twelve years old. His face was almost too dark to see, which came of him standing in the shadow of a building, and having very brown skin; but he looked happy, merry indeed…perhaps at the thought of having routed the lowlifes; and his bearing as he stood before them had nothing clownish or rude about it.

"I saw them," he went on, "as I came up; and I'm very glad I did. I knew they were after somebody, but I couldn't see who it was. They won't touch you so long as I'm with you."

"Why, who are you?" asked the nurse, offended at the freedom with which he spoke to them.

"I'm the Earl's son."

"Who's the Earl?"

"The Earl of the Mission."

"I don't know him."

"I'm his son, though."

"And why should the lowlifes mind you?"

"Because I don't mind them. I'm used to them."

"What difference does that make?"

"If you're not afraid of them, they're afraid of you. I'm not afraid of them. That's all. But it's all what's wanted...up here, that is. It's a different thing down there. They won't always mind that rap, even down there. And if anyone sings it, they stand grinning at him awfully; and if he gets frightened, and misses a word, or says a wrong one, they...oh! Don't they give it to him!"

"What do they do to him?" asked Tiffany, with a trembling voice.

"Don't go frightening the young lady," said the nurse.

"The young lady!" repeated the little boy, taking off his curious cap. "I beg your pardon; but you oughtn't to be out so late. Everybody knows that's too dangerous for the likes of you."

"Yes, indeed it is!" said the nurse, beginning to cry again. "And I shall have to suffer for it."

"What does that matter?" said the boy. "It must be your fault. It is the little lady who will suffer for it. I hope they didn't get a good look at her. If they did, they're sure to know her again: they're awfully sharp."

"Nursie! Nursie!" cried the little rich girl. "Take me home."

"Don't go on like that," said the nurse to the boy, almost fiercely. "How could I help it? I lost my way."

"You shouldn't have been out so late. You wouldn't have lost your way if you hadn't been frightened," said the boy. "Come on. I'll show you the way. Shall I carry the little lady?"

"Impertinence!" murmured the nurse, but she did not say it aloud, for she thought if she made him angry he might take his revenge by telling someone belonging to the house, and then it would be sure to come to Tiffany's father's ears.

"No, thank you," said Tiffany. "I can walk very well, though I can't run so fast as Nursie. If you will give me one hand, Nursie will give me another, and then I shall get on famously."

They soon had her between them, holding a hand of each.

"Now let's run," said the nurse.

"No, no," said the little boy. "That's the worst thing you can do. If you hadn't run before, you would not have lost your way. And if you run now, they will be after you in a moment."

"I don't want to run," said Tiffany.

"You don't think of me," said the nurse.

"Yes, I do, Nursie. The boy says they won't touch us if we don't run."

"Yes, but if they know at the house that I've kept you out so late I shall be turned away, and that would break my heart."

"Turned away, Nursie! Who would turn you away?"

"Your father, child."

"But I'll tell him it was all my fault. And you know it was, Nursie."

"He won't mind that. I'm sure he won't."

"Then I'll cry, and go down on my knees to him, and beg him not to take away my own dear Nursie."

The nurse was comforted at hearing this, and said no more. They went on, walking pretty fast, but taking care not to run a step.

"I want to talk to you," said Tiffany to the little boy; "but it's so awkward! I don't know your name."

"My name's Jonny, little lady."

"What a funny name! Jonny! What more?"

"Jonny Mo. What's your name, please?"

"Tiffany."

"What more?"

"I don't know what more. What more is my name, Nursie?"

"Young ladies haven't got to worry about more than one name at your age. They don't want the problems."

"Oh, then, Jonny, you must call me just Tiffany and no more."

"No, indeed," said the nurse indignantly. "He shall do no such thing."

"What shall he call me, then, Nursie?"

"Missie, or Mam."

"Missie! What's that? No, no, Nursie. I won't be called names.

I don't like them. You told me once yourself it's only rude children that call names; and I'm sure Jonny wouldn't be rude. Jonny, my name's Tiffany."

"Well, Tiffany," said Jonny Mo, with a glance at the nurse which showed he enjoyed teasing her, "it is very kind of you to let me call you anything. I like your name a lot."

He expected the nurse to interfere again; but he soon saw that she was too frightened to speak. She was staring at something a few yards before them in the middle of the road, where it narrowed between buildings so that only one could pass at a time.

"It is very much kinder of you to go out of your way to take us home," said Tiffany.

"I'm not going out my way yet," said Jonny. "It's on the other side of those buildings the road turns off to my dad's."

"You wouldn't think of leaving us till we're safe home, I'm sure," gasped the nurse.

"Of course not," said Jonny.

"You dear, good, kind Jonny! I'll give you a kiss when we get home," said the little rich girl.

The nurse gave her a great pull by the hand she held. But at that instant the something in the middle of the way, which had looked like a great lump of garbage thrown down from one of the dark windows above, began to move. One after another it shot out four long things, like two arms and two legs, but it was now too dark to tell what they were. The nurse began to tremble from head to foot. Tiffany clasped Jonny's hand yet faster, and Jonny began to sing again:

"One, two…
I'll smash you!
Three, four…
Your mama's a whore!
Five, six…
You want a fix!

Seven, eight...
Hold your arm straight!
Nine, ten...
I'll hit ya again!
Hurry! Scurry!
There's a toad
In the road!
Smash it!
Squash it!
Fry it!
Dry it!
Ooooo...I'm bad!"

As he uttered the last words, Jonny let go his hold of his companion, and rushed at the thing in the road as if he would trample it under his feet. It gave a great spring, and ran straight up one of the debris boxes next to the old building like a huge spider. Jonny turned back laughing, and took Tiffany's hand again. She grasped his very tight, but said nothing till they had passed the buildings. A few yards more and she found herself on a part of the road she knew, and was able to speak again.

"Do you know, Jonny, I don't quite like your song: it sounds to me rather rude," she said.

"Yeah, maybe it is," answered Jonny. "I never thought of that; but it works. We do it because they don't like it."

"Who don't like it?"

"The lowlifes, as we call them."

"Don't!" said the nurse.

"Why not?" said Jonny.

"I beg you don't. Please don't."

"Oh! If you ask me that way, sure, I won't; though I don't know why. Look! There are the lights of your part of town. You'll be at home in five minutes now."

Nothing more happened. They reached home in safety. Nobody had missed them, or even known they had gone out; and they arrived at the door belonging to their part of the house without anyone seeing them. The nurse was rushing in with a hurried and not over-gracious good night to Jonny; but the little rich girl pulled her hand from hers, and was just throwing her arms round Jonny's neck, when she caught her again and dragged her away.

"Nursie! Nursie! I promised a kiss," cried Tiffany.

"A young lady mustn't give kisses. It's not at all proper," said the nurse.

"But I promised," said the little rich girl.

"There's no occasion; he's only a poor black boy."

"He's a good boy, and a brave boy, and he has been very kind to us. Nursie! Nursie! I promised."

"Then you shouldn't have promised."

"Nursie, I promised him a kiss."

"Young lady," said the nurse, suddenly grown very respectful, "You must come in directly."

"Nurse, a young lady must not break her word," said Tiffany, drawing herself up and standing stock-still.

Nursie did not know which the father might count the worst…to let the little rich girl be out after sunset, or to let her kiss a black boy. She did not know that, being a gentleman, as many rich men have been, he would have counted neither of them the worse. However much he might have disliked his daughter to kiss the black boy, he would not have had her break her word for all the lowlifes in creation. But, as I said, the nurse was not lady enough to understand this, and so she was in a great difficulty, for, if she insisted, someone might hear the little rich girl cry and run to see, and then all would come out. But here Jonny came again to the rescue.

"Never mind, Tiffany," he said. "It ain't a good idea for you to kiss me tonight. But you won't have to break your word. I'll come another time. You can bet I will…just tell your nurse to stop calling me a 'boy'!"

"Oh, thank you, Jonny!" said the little rich girl, as she stopped crying. "I'll make sure she never says that again."

"Good night, Tiffany; good night, Nursie," said Jonny, and turned and was out of sight in a moment.

"I should like to see him!" muttered the nurse, as she carried the little rich girl to the nursery.

"You will see him," said Tiffany. "You may be sure Jonny will keep his word. He's sure to come again."

"I should like to see him!" repeated the nurse, and said no more. She did not want to open a new cause of strife with the little rich girl by saying more plainly what she meant. Glad enough that she had succeeded both in getting home unseen, and in keeping the little rich girl from kissing the black boy, she resolved to watch her far better in the future. Her carelessness had already doubled the danger she was in. Formerly the lowlifes were her only fear; now she had to protect her charge from Jonny as well.

Chapter 7

Jonny went home whistling. He resolved to say nothing about the little rich girl for fear of getting the nurse into trouble, for while he enjoyed teasing her because of her absurdity, he was careful not to do her any harm. He saw no more of the lowlifes, and was soon fast asleep in his bed.

He woke in the middle of the night, and thought he heard some curious noises outside. He sat up and listened; then got up, and, opening the door very quietly, went out. When he peeped round the corner, he saw, under his own window, a group of stumpy creatures, whom he at once recognized by their shape and smell. Hardly, however, had he begun his "One, two, three!" when they broke asunder, scurried away, and were out of sight. He returned laughing, got into bed again, and was fast asleep in a moment.

Reflecting a little over the matter in the morning, he came to the conclusion that, as nothing of the kind had ever happened before, they must be annoyed with him for interfering to protect the little rich girl. By the time he was dressed, however, he was thinking of something quite different, for he did not value the enmity of the lowlifes in the least.

As soon as they had had breakfast, he set off with his father for work.

They entered the underground parking garage by the elevator opening in Civic Center Plaza, where all the office workers came out after parking their fancy cars. They went down several floors, then followed a side passage that sloped steeply into the heart of the massive underground complex. With many angles and windings and branchings-off, and sometimes with steps where it came upon a trench, it led them deep into the earth below the city before they arrived at the place where they had a little locker where they could change their clothing. Then Jonny went back up a few floors to where he washed cars while his father worked to keep the complex air conditioning and electric systems running. There were various kinds of cars here, for the garage was where many rich people parked in the better sorts of autos. With Jags and Cads, and Rolls, he pulled them forward, then got them wet, and was soon hard at work with sponge and shammy. Father and son were at work near each other, but not in the same crew...the passages in which his father worked were far below Jonny, sometimes uncomfortably cramped. If they stopped for a moment they could hear everywhere around them, some nearer, some farther off, the sounds of their companions working away in all directions in the inside of the great complex...some washing cars, some removing sections of rotten old pipes, others parking cars, others patching bad spots in the cement walls. Sometimes, if the worker was in a very lonely part, he would hear only the breathing of the air conditioning system, no louder than that of the purr of a cat, for the sound would come from a great distance off through the solid concrete construction.

The work was hard at best, for it is very warm underground; but it was not particularly unpleasant, and some of the men, when they wanted to earn a little more money for a particular purpose, would stop behind the rest and work all night on overtime. But you could not tell night from day down there, except from feeling tired and sleepy; for no light of the sun ever came into those gloomy regions. Some who had thus remained behind during the night, although certain there were none of their companions at work, would declare the next morning that they heard, every time they halted for a moment to take breath, movements all about them, as if the complex were then more full of workers than ever it was during the day; and some in consequence would never stay overnight, for all knew those were the sounds of the lowlifes. They worked only at night, for the workers' night was the lowlifes' day. Indeed, the greater number of the workers were afraid of the lowlifes; for there were strange stories well known amongst them of the treatment some had received whom the lowlifes had surprised at their work during the night. The more courageous of them, however, amongst them Earl Mo and Jonny, who in this took after his father, had stayed in the garage all night again and again, and although they had several times encountered a few stray lowlifes, had never yet failed in driving them away. As I have indicated already, the chief defense against them was loud verse, for they hated verse of every kind, and some kinds (such as "rap") they could not endure at all. I suspect they could not make any themselves, and that was why they disliked it so much. At all events, those who were most afraid of them were those who could neither make verses themselves nor remember the verses that other people made for them; while those who were never afraid were those who could make verses for themselves; for although there were certain old rhymes which were very effectual, yet it was well know that a new rhyme, if of the right sort, was even more distasteful to them, and therefore more effectual in putting them to flight.

Perhaps my readers may be wondering what the lowlifes could be about, working all night long, seeing they never seemed to work in the day; but when I have informed them concerning what Jonny learned the very next night, they will be able to understand.

For Jonny had determined, if his father would permit him, to remain there alone this night...and that for two reasons: first, he wanted to get extra wages by washing all the rich people's cars who went to the opera so that he might buy a very warm coat for his mother, who had begun to complain of the cold of the city air sooner than usual this autumn; and second, he had just a faint hope of finding out what the lowlifes were about under his window the night before.

When he told his father, he made no objection, for he had great confidence in his boy's courage and resources.

"I'm sorry I can't stay with you," said Earl, "but I want to go and pay the parson a visit this evening, and besides I've had a bit of a headache all day."

"I'm sorry for that dad," said Jonny.

"Oh! It's not that bad. You'll be sure to take care of yourself, won't you?"

"Yes, Father; I will. I'll keep a sharp look-out, I promise you."

Jonny was the only one who remained in the second level work station of the garage. About six o'clock the rest went away, everyone bidding him good night, and telling him to take care of himself; for he was a great favourite with them all.

"Don't forget your raps," said one.

"No, no," answered Jonny.

"It's no matter if he does," said another, "for he'll only have to make a new one."

"Yes: but he mightn't be able to make it fast or loud enough," said another; "And while it was cooking in his head, they might take the advantage and smash the hell out of him."

"I'll do my best," said Jonny. "I'm not afraid."

"We all know that," they returned, and left him.

Chapter 8

For some time Jonny worked away briskly, parking all the clean cars he had just worked on behind him, to be ready for giving back to the rich people as they came to pick them up. He heard a good deal of lowlife noise, but it all sounded far away in the other levels, and he paid it little heed. Towards midnight he began to feel rather hungry; so he dropped his hose, got out a lump of French bread which in the morning he had laid in a box where he kept soap and wax, sat down on an old folding chair, and ate his supper. Then he leaned back for five minutes' rest before beginning his work again, and laid his head against the wall. He had not kept the position for one minute before he heard something which made him sharpen his ears. It sounded like a voice inside the cement. After a while he heard it again. It was a lowlife voice...there could be no doubt about that...and this time he could make out the words.

"Hadn't we better be moving?" it said.

A rougher and deeper voice replied:

"There's no hurry. That wretched little brat won't be through tonight, if he works ever so hard. He's not by any means going to get around here."

"But you still think the parts will be worth dragging through our house?" asked the first voice.

"Yes, but he will never see it missing. If he had picked it up first," said the lowlife, tapping something metallic, "he might have noticed it gone; but he's too busy now over there, and if he keeps working on the short-time parkers it will be a week before he finds the empty space. Still, perhaps, in case of accident it would be as well to be getting out of this. Fingers, you'll take the tools. That's your business, you know."

"Yea, man," said a third voice. "But you must help me to get the chest on my back. It's awfully heavy, you know."

"Well, it ain't just a bag of smoke, I admit. But you're as strong as a Kenworth, Fingers."

"You say so, man. I think myself I'm all right. But I could carry ten times as much if it wasn't for my feet."

"That is your weak point, I confess, my boy."

"Ain't it yours, too, man?"

"Well, to be honest, it is a lowlife weakness. Why they come so rotten, I declare I haven't an idea."

"'Specially when your head's so hard, you know, man."

"Yes, my boy. The lowlife's glory is his head. To think how the fellows up above there have to put on helmets and things when they go exploring or fighting! Ha! Ha!"

"But why don't we wear shoes like them, Father? I should like it ...especially when I've got a chest of tools like that on my back."

"Well, you see, it's not the fashion. I've heard that the greatest, richest business man in the city above hates shoes! He hardly ever wears shoes."

"His wife does."

"Yes, but that's for distinction. His first wife, you see...I mean the Big Man's first wife...wore shoes, of course, because she came from a rich family; and so, when she died, the next wife would not be inferior to her as she called it, and would wear fancy shoes, too. It was all pride. She is the hardest in forbidding them to poor people."

"I'm sure I wouldn't wear them... no, not for...that I wouldn't!" said the first voice, which was evidently that of a woman. "I can't think why either of them should."

"Didn't I tell you the first was rich?" said the other. "That was the only silly thing I ever knew the Big Man guilty of. Why should he marry an outlandish woman like that...one of our natural enemies, too?"

"I suppose he fell in love with her."

"Pooh! Pooh! He's just as happy now with one of his own people."

"Did she die very soon? They didn't tease her to death, did they?"

"Oh, dear, no! The Big Man worshiped her very footmarks."

"What made her die, then? Didn't the fog agree with her?"

"She died when the daughter was born."

"How silly of her! We never do that. It must have been because she wore shoes."

"I don't know that."

"Why do they wear shoes up there?"

"Ah, now that's a sensible question, and I will answer it. But in order to do so, I must first tell you a secret. I once saw the Big Man's wife's feet."

"Without her shoes?"

"Yes...without her shoes."

"No! Did you? How was it?"

"Never you mind how it was. She didn't know I saw them. And what do you think!...they had healthy toes!"

"Toes! What's that?"

"You may well ask! I should never have known if I had not seen the rich woman's feet and then been reminded. I had not had healthy toes since Nam. Just imagine! The ends of her feet were split up into five pieces with no rot between!"

"Oh, horrid! How could the rich man have fallen in love with her?"

"You forget that she wore shoes. That is just why she wore them. That is why all the men, and women, too, up there wear shoes. They can't bear the sight of their own feet without them."

"Ah! Now I understand. If ever you wish for toes again, Fingers, I'll hit your feet...I will."

"No, no, Mother; please don't."

"Then don't you."

"But with such a big box on my back…"

A horrid scream followed, which Jonny interpreted as in reply to a blow from the mother upon the feet of her eldest lowlife. Jonny looked around at that point and realized that the voices were coming through the air conditioning duct that had an opening just over his head.

"Well, I never knew so much before!" remarked a fourth voice.

"Your knowledge is not universal quite yet," said the father. "You were only fifteen last month. Mind you see to the dashboard and rugs. As soon as we've finished our supper, we'll be up and going. Ha! Ha! Ha!"

"What are you laughing at, husband?"

"I'm laughing to think what a mess the daytime workers will find themselves in…somewhere before this day in ten days or so."

"Why, what do you mean?"

"Oh, nothing."

"Oh, yes, you do mean something. You always do mean something."

"It's more than you do, then, wife."

"That may be; but it's not more than I find out, you know."

"Ha! Ha! You're a sharp one. What a mother you've got, Fingers!"

"Yes, Father."

"Well, I suppose I must tell you. They're all at the palace consulting about it tonight; and as soon as we've got away from this place I'm going there to hear what night they fix upon. I should like to see that young ruffian there on the other side, struggling in the agonies of…"

He dropped his voice so low that Jonny could hear only a growl. The growl went on in the low bass for a good while, as inarticulate as if the lowlife's tongue had been a sausage; and it was not until his wife spoke again that it rose to its former pitch.

"But what shall we do when you are at the palace?" she asked.

"I will see you safe in the hole first. Tonto, you mind the other parts...and you get the engine parts."

After this arose a confused conversation about the various goods and their transport; and Jonny heard nothing more that was of any importance.

He now knew at least one of the reasons for the constant sound of the lowlifes at night. They were stealing car parts from the parked cars. But he had learned two things of far greater importance. The first was, that some grievous calamity was preparing and almost ready to fall upon the heads of the workers in the garage complex; the second was...the one weak point of a lowlife's body; he had not known that their feet were so tender as he had now reason to suspect. He had heard it said that many of them had no toes: he had never had opportunity of inspecting them closely enough, in the dusk in which they always appeared, to satisfy himself as to whether they had no fingers, although that also was commonly said to be the fact. One of the garage men, indeed, who had had more schooling than the rest, was wont to argue that such must have been the primordial condition of humanity, and that education and handicraft had developed both toes and fingers...with which proposition Jonny had once heard his father sarcastically agree, alleging in support of it the probability that babies' gloves were a traditional remnant of the old state of things; while the stockings of all ages, no regard being paid in them to the toes, pointed in the same direction. But what was of importance was the fact concerning the softness of the lowlife feet, which he foresaw might be useful to all daylight people. What he had to do in the meantime, however, was to discover, if possible, the special evil design the lowlifes had now in their heads.

Although he knew all the work crews and all the levels where they worked and communicated, he had not the least idea where the palace of the king of the lowlifes was; otherwise he would have set out at once on the enterprise of discovering what the said design was. He judged, and rightly, that it must lie in a farther part of the underground labyrinths of the city. There must be some way in, however; for the lowlifes he had just heard were in the garage and about to leave. If only he could get to them in time to follow as they retreated! A quick run would doubtless be sufficient...just down the next level where the ducting led; but if he attempted to run too fast when the garage was this quiet they would hear him, and he would only hasten the departure of the family, put them on their guard, and perhaps lose their involuntary guidance. He therefore began to walk very slowly, and soon found the old stairway that went down the back wall that he could creep down very quietly.

Reaching the bottom of the last step, Jonny carefully opened the old firedoor to the lowest level of the garage.

"What was that noise?" said the lowlife father.

Jonny didn't move; didn't even breathe.

"It must be that one brat that stayed behind the rest," said the mother.

"No, he's been gone a good while. I haven't heard the hose running for an hour. Besides, it wasn't like that."

"Then I suppose it must have been a rat or something."

"Perhaps. It will have more to feed on soon."

Jonny kept quite still. After a little while, hearing nothing but the sounds of their preparations for departure, mingled with an occasional word of direction, and anxious to know whether the reopening of the door would give him away, he put his hand through the opening to feel. It went in a good way, and then came in contact with something soft. He had but a moment to feel it over, it was so quickly withdrawn: it was one of the toeless rotten lowlife feet. The owner of it gave a cry of fright.

"What's the matter, Fingers?" asked the mother.

"A beast came out of the stairwell and licked my foot."

"Nonsense! There are no wild beasts in this part of the city," said his father.

"But it was, Father. I felt it."

"Nonsense, I say. Will you malign your native realms and reduce them to a level with the city above? That is swarming with dogs and beasts of every description."

"But I did feel it, Father."

"I tell you to hold your tongue. You are no patriot."

Jonny suppressed his laughter, and lay still as a mouse...but no stiller, for every moment he kept pushing the door a little more with his fingers. He was slowly making the opening bigger, pushing the door further open.

There seemed to be a good many in the family, to judge from the mass of confused talk which now and then came through the opening; but when all were speaking together, and just as if they had frogs in their throats, it was not easy to make out much that was said. At length he heard once more what the father lowlife was saying.

"Now, then," he said, "get your bundles on your backs. Here, Fingers, I'll help you up with the chest."

"I wish it was my chest, Father."

"Your turn will come in good time enough! Make haste. I must go to the meeting at the palace tonight. When that's over, we can come back and clear out the last of the morning. Now turn on your glow lights, and come along. What a distinction it is to provide our own light, instead of being dependent on a thing hung up in the air...a most disagreeable contrivance...intended no doubt to blind us when we venture out under its baleful influence! Quite glaring and vulgar, I call it, though no doubt useful to poor creatures who haven't the wit to make light for themselves!"

Jonny could hardly keep himself from calling through to know how they made the strange green light that now glowed from little sticks that each of them carried. But a moment's reflection showed him that they would have said they did, inasmuch as they broke a tiny chemical flask inside each plastic stick, and the light came.

Chapter 9

A sound of many soft feet followed, but soon ceased. Then Jonny flew at the door like a tiger, and pushed it open wide. He would not betray himself by turning on his own small flashlight, but the glow of the retreating company, which he found departing in a straight line up a long-forgotten PG&E trench, threw back light enough to afford him a glance round the deserted area where they had been. To his surprise, he could discover nothing to distinguish it from an ordinary empty parking spot in the garage, many of which he had seen before. The lowlifes had talked of coming back for the rest of their things: he saw nothing that would have made him suspect they or anything else had been there. The floor was rough and covered with oil spots; the walls full of rough cement corners; the roof like it was on all the other levels; while on one side the trench, no thicker than a big man's shoulders, pointed off into the unseen distance. But the troop in front of him was toiling under heavy burdens. He could distinguish Fingers now and then, in the flickering light and shade, with his heavy red chest on his bending shoulders; while the second brother was almost buried in what looked like a great bag of odd parts, including several car fenders. "How did they pull an entire car apart?" thought Jonny; but in a moment the troop disappeared at a turn of the way, and it was now both safe and necessary for Jonny to follow them, lest they should be round the next turning before he saw them again, for so he might lose them altogether. He darted after them like a greyhound. When he reached the corner and looked cautiously round, he saw them again at some distance down another long passage. None of the galleries he saw that night bore signs of the work of man in years...or of lowlife either. Pipes, far older than any he had ever seen before, hung from their roofs; and their floors were rough with years of dust and dirt and stones. He waited again at this corner till they had disappeared round the next, and so followed them a long way through one passage after another. The passages grew more and more lofty, and were more and more covered in the roof with shining stalactites.

It was a strange enough procession which he followed. But the strangest part of it was the animals which crowded amongst the feet of the lowlifes. It was true they had no wild animals down there...at least they did not know of any; but they had a wonderful number of tame ones. I must, however, reserve any contributions towards the natural history of these for a later position in my story.

At length, turning a corner too abruptly, he had almost rushed into the middle of the lowlife family; for there they had already set down all their burdens on the floor of a chamber considerably larger than any he had seen so far. They were as yet too breathless to speak, else he would have had warning of the halt. He started back, however, before anyone saw him, and retreating a good way, stood watching till the father should come out to go to the palace. Before very long, both he and his son Fingers appeared and kept on in the same direction as before, while Jonny followed them again with renewed precaution. For a long time he heard no sound except something like the rush of a river inside the earth; but at length, what seemed the far-off noise of a great shouting reached his ears, which, however, presently ceased. After advancing a good way farther, he thought he heard a single voice. It sounded way clearer, and clearer as he went on, until at last he could almost distinguish the words. In a moment or two, keeping after the lowlifes round another corner, he once more started back...this time in amazement.

Tiffany and the Lowlifes

He was at the entrance of a magnificent cavern. Of an oval shape, once probably a huge manmade reservoir of water or fuel, now the great palace hall of the lowlifes. It rose to a tremendous height, but the roof was composed of such shining materials and the multitude of glow lights carried by the lowlifes who crowded the floor lighted up the place so brilliantly, that Jonny could see the top quite well. But he had no idea how immense the place was until his eyes had got accustomed to it, which was not for a good many minutes. The rough projections on the walls, and the shadows thrown upwards from them by the glow lights, made the sides of the chamber look as if they were crowded with statues upon brackets and pedestals, reaching in irregular tiers from floor to roof. The walls themselves were, in many parts, of brick cover with gloriously shining substances, some of them gorgeously coloured besides, which powerfully contrasted with the shadows. Jonny could not help wondering whether his rhymes would be of any use against such a multitude of lowlifes as filled the floor of the hall, and indeed felt considerably tempted to begin his shout of "One, two, three!" but as there was no reason for routing them, and much for endeavouring to discover their designs, he kept himself perfectly quiet, and peeping round the edge of the doorway, listened with both his sharp ears.

At the other end of the hall, high above the heads of the multitude, was a terrace-like ledge of considerable height, caused by the receding of the upper part of the cavern wall and some age-old machinery. Upon this sat the king and his court, the king on a throne made of what looked to be tons of green copper, and his court upon lower seats around it. The king had been making them a speech, and the applause which followed it was what Jonny had heard. One of the court was now addressing the multitude. What he heard him say was to the following effect:

"Hence it appears that two plans have been for some time together working in the strong head of His Majesty for the deliverance of his people. Regardless of the fact that we were the first possessors of the regions they now inhabit, regardless equally of the fact that we abandoned that region from the loftiest motives; regardless also of the self-evident fact that we excel them so far in mental ability as they excel us in stature, they look upon us as a degraded race, and make a mockery of all our finer feelings. But the time has almost arrived when...thanks to His Majesty's inventive genius...it will be in our power to take a thorough revenge upon them once and for all, in respect of their unfriendly behaviour."

"May it please Your Majesty..." cried a voice close by the door, which Jonny recognized as that of the lowlife he had followed.

"Who is he that interrupts the Chancellor?" cried another from near the throne.

"Wrecker," answered several voices.

"He is our trusty subject," said the king himself, in a slow and stately voice: "Let him come forward and speak."

A lane was parted through the crowd, and Wrecker, having ascended the platform and bowed to the king, spoke as follows:

"Sire, I would have held my peace, had I not known that I only knew how near was the moment to which the Chancellor had just referred. In all probability, before another day is past, the enemy will have broken through into my main storage den...the partition between being even now not more than a few feet in thickness between my parts and the PG&E crews."

"He must mean the new utility tunnel under downtown," thought Jonny to himself.

"This very evening I have had to remove my fender storage; therefore, the sooner we are ready to carry out the plan, for the execution of which His Majesty has been making such magnificent preparations, the better. I may just add, that within the last few days I have perceived a small outbreak in my dining room, which, combined with observations upon the course of the main Bay sewer river, has convinced me that close to the spot must lie a deeper pipe in its channel. This discovery will, I trust, add considerably to the otherwise immense forces at His Majesty's disposal."

He ceased, and the king graciously acknowledged his speech with a bend of his head; whereupon Wrecker, after a bow to His Majesty, slid down amongst the rest of the undistinguished multitude. Then the Chancellor rose and resumed.

"The information which the worthy Wrecker has given us," he said, "might have been of considerable import at the present moment, but for that other design already referred to, which naturally takes precedence. His Majesty, unwilling to proceed to extremities, and well aware that such measures sooner or later result in violent reactions, has excogitated a more fundamental and comprehensive measure, of which I need say no more. Should His Majesty be successful...as who dares to doubt?...then a peace, all to the advantage of the lowlife kingdom, will be established for a generation at least, rendered absolutely secure by the pledge which His Royal Highness the prince will have and hold for the good behaviour of her relatives. Should His Majesty fail...which who shall dare even to imagine in his most secret thought?...then will be the time for carrying out with rigour the design to which Wrecker referred, and for which our preparations are even now all but completed. The failure of the former will render the latter imperative."

Jonny, perceiving that the assembly was drawing to a close and that there was little chance of either plan being more fully discovered, now thought it prudent to make his escape before the lowlifes began to disperse, and slipped quietly away.

There was not much danger of meeting any lowlifes, for all the men at least were left behind him in the palace; but there was considerable danger of his taking a wrong turning, for he had now no light, and had therefore to depend upon him memory and his hands. After he had left behind him the glow that issued from the door of Wrecker's abode, he was utterly without guide, so far as his eyes were concerned.

He was most anxious to get back through the trench before the lowlifes should return to fetch the remains of their business. It was not that he was in the least afraid of them, but, as it was of the utmost importance that he should thoroughly discover what the plans they were cherishing were, he must not occasion the slightest suspicion that they were watched by a daytimer.

He hurried on, feeling his way along the walls of rock. Had he not been very courageous, he must have been very anxious, for he could not but know that if he lost his way it would be the most difficult thing in the world to find it again. Morning would bring no light into these regions; and towards him least of all, who was known as a special rapster and persecutor, could lowlifes be expected to exercise courtesy. Well might he wish that he had brought his large flashlight, of which he had not thought when he crept so eagerly after the lowlifes! His little one had stopped working. He wished it all the more when, after a while, he found his way blocked up, and could get no farther. It was of no use to turn back, for he had not the least idea where he had begun to go wrong. Mechanically, however, he kept feeling about the walls that hemmed him in. His hand came upon a place where a tiny stream of water was running down the face of the cement. "What a stupid I am!" he said to himself. "I am actually at the end of my journey! And there are the lowlifes coming back to fetch their things!" he added, as the green glimmer of their glow lights appeared at the end of the long trench that led up to the back of the garage's lowest level. In a moment he had thrown himself on the floor, and wriggled around a parked car and into the once-locked door. The floor on the other side was several feet lower, which made it easier to get up over the ledge onto the parking ramp. It was all he could do to shut the door quickly enough, but he did manage to push it again. He sat down on the steps and thought.

He was pretty sure that the latter plan of the lowlifes was to inundate the lower levels of the city by breaking outlets for the water accumulated in the sewers. While the part hollowed by the new PG&E tunnel remained shut off from that inhabited by the lowlifes, they had had no opportunity of injuring them thus; but now that a passage was broken through, and the lowlifes' part proved the higher, it was clear to Jonny that the daytimers could be destroyed in an hour. Water was always the chief danger to which underground constructions were exposed. They met with a little flooding every now and then, and hence they were careful as soon as they saw any appearance of water.

As the result of his reflections while the lowlifes were busy in their business, it seemed to Jonny that it would be best to build up the whole of his crew, filling the PG&E tunnel in with stone, and clay or lime, so that there should be no smallest channel for the water to get into. There was not, however, any immediate danger, for the execution of the lowlifes' plan was contingent upon the failure of that unknown design which was to take precedence of it; and he was most anxious to keep the door of communication open, that he might if possible discover what the former plan was. At the same time they could not resume their intermitted labours for the inundation without his finding it out; when by putting all hands to the work, the one existing outlet and the PG&E tunnel might in a single night be rendered impenetrable to any weight of water; for by filling the lowlife tunnel entirely up, their embankment would be buttressed by the sides of other structures and the earth itself.

As soon as he found that the lowlifes had again retired, he locked the door of the stairwell. He then thought it better, as he might have occasion to be up a good many nights after this, to go home and have some sleep.

How pleasant the night air felt upon the outside of the garage after what he had gone through underground! He hurried up the hill without meeting a single lowlife on the way, and called and tapped at the window until he woke his father, who soon rose and let him in. He told him the whole story, and, just as he had expected, his father thought it best to warn the PG&E men, but at the same time to pretend occasionally to be at work there still in order that the lowlifes might have no suspicions. He would call his boss in the morning. Both father and son then went to bed and slept soundly until the sun came up.

Chapter 10

The weather continued fine for weeks, and the little rich girl went out every day. So long a period of fine weather had indeed never been known in the City. The only uncomfortable thing was that her nurse was so nervous and particular about being in before the sun was down that often she would take to her heels when nothing worse than a fleecy cloud crossing the sun threw a shadow on the buildings; and many an evening they were home a full hour before the sunlight had left the weather-cock on the roof of the house. If it had not been for such odd behaviour Tiffany would by this time have almost forgotten the lowlifes. She never forgot Jonny, but him she remembered for his own sake, and indeed would have remembered him if only because a lady never forgets her debts until they are paid.

One splendid sunshiny day, about an hour after noon, Tiffany, who was playing on a lawn in the garden, heard the distant blast of a horn. She jumped up with a cry of joy, for she knew by that particular blast that her father was on his way to see her. This part of the garden lay on the slope of the hill and allowed a full view of the Marina and bay below. So she shaded her eyes with her hand and looked far away to catch the first glimpse of the shining car coming up the road. Again came the horn-blast which was to her like the voice of her father calling across the distance: "Tiffany, I'm coming." On and on the car came until she could clearly distinguish the rich man in the back seat. It was a long time since he had been to see her, and her little heart beat faster and faster as the shining car approached, for she loved her father very dearly and was nowhere so happy as in his arms. When they reached a certain point, after which she could see the car no more from the garden, she ran to the gate, and there stood till up it drove and honked with one more bright horn-blast which said: "Tiffany, I am home."

By this time the people of the house were all gathered at the gate, but Tiffany stood alone in front of them. When the car pulled up she ran to the side of the white metal and held up her arms. The rich man opened the door and took her hands. In an instant she was on the leather seat and clasped in his great strong arms. I wish I could describe the rich man so that you could see him in your mind. He had gentle, blue eyes, but a nose that made him look like an eagle. Hair streaked with silvery lines flowed fully on his head, and as Tiffany sat on his lap and hid her glad face upon his shoulder it mingled with the golden hair which her mother had given her, and the two together were like a cloud with streaks of the sun woven through it. After he had held her to his heart for a minute he spoke to his driver, and the great beautiful car, which had been charging up the road so proudly a little while before, crept gently through the gate and up to the door of the house. Then the rich man helped her out of the car and, getting out himself, took her hand and walked with her into the entrance hall and the Great Hall, which was hardly ever entered except when he came to see his little daughter. There he sat down, with two of his counselors who had accompanied him, to have some refreshment, and Tiffany sat on his right hand and drank her milk out of a curiously carved cup.

After the rich man had eaten and drunk he turned to the little rich girl and said, stroking her hair:

"Now, my child, what shall we do next?"

This was the question he almost always put to her first after their meal together; and Tiffany had been waiting for it with some impatience, for now, she thought, she should be able to settle a question which constantly perplexed her.

"I should like you to take me to see my great old grandmother."

The king looked grave and said:

"What does my little daughter mean?"

"I mean the Lady Tiffany that lives up in the roof...the very old lady, you know, with the long hair of silver."

The rich man only gazed at his little daughter with a look which she could not understand.

"She's got her money and good furniture in her bedroom," she went on; "but I've not been in there yet. You know she's there, don't you?"

"No," said the rich man, very quietly.

"Then it must all be a dream," said Tiffany. "I half thought it was; but I couldn't be sure. Now I am sure of it. Besides, I couldn't find her the next time I went up."

At that moment a snow-white pigeon flew in at an open window and settled upon Tiffany's head. She broke into a merry laugh, cowered a little, and put up her hands to her head, saying:

"Dear dovey, don't peck me. You'll pull out my hair with your long claws if you don't mind."

The rich man stretched out his hand to take the pigeon, but it spread its wings and flew again through the open window, when its whiteness made one flash in the sun and vanished. The rich man laid his hand on his daughter's head, held it back a little, gazed in her face, smiled half a smile, and sighed half a sigh.

"Come, my child; we'll have a walk in the garden together," he said.

"You won't come up and see my huge, great beautiful grandmother, then, Papa?" said the little rich girl.

"Not this time," said her father very gently. "She has not invited me, you know, and great old ladies like her do not choose to be visited without leave asked and given."

The garden was a very lovely place. Being upon a hillside where reality blended into the roof of her childhood world, there were areas in it where faux rocks came through in great masses, and all immediately about them remained quite wild. Tufts of heather grew upon them, and other hardy mountain plants and flowers, while near them would be lovely roses and lilies and all pleasant garden flowers. This mingling of the wild world with the civilized world was very quaint, and it was impossible for any number of gardeners to make such a garden look formal and stiff.

Against one of these faux rocks was a garden seat, shadowed from the afternoon sun by the overhanging of the rock itself. There was a little winding path up the top of the rock, and on top another seat; but they sat on the seat at its foot because the sun was so hot; and there they talked together of many things. At length the rich man said:

"You were out late one evening, Tiffany."

"Yes, Papa. It was my fault; and Nursie was very sorry."

"I must talk to your nurse about it," said the rich man.

"Don't speak loud to her, please, Papa," said Tiffany. "She's been so afraid of being late ever since! Indeed she has not been naughty. It was only a mistake for once."

"Once might be too often," murmured the rich man to himself, as he stroked his child's head.

I can't tell you how he had come to know. I am sure Jonny had not told him. Someone about the house must have seen them, after all. He sat for a good while thinking. There was no sound to be heard except that of a little stream which ran merrily out of an opening in the rock by where they sat, and sped away down the hill through the garden. Then he rose and, leaving Tiffany where she was, went into the house and sent for the nurse, with whom he had a talk that made her cry.

When in the evening he drove away inside his great white car, he left six of his attendants behind him, with orders that three of them should watch outside the house every night, walking round and round it from sunset to sunrise. It was clear he was not quite comfortable about the little rich girl.

Chapter 11

Nothing more happened worth telling for some time. The autumn came and went by. There were no more flowers in the garden. The wind blew strong, and howled among the rocks. The rain fell, and drenched the few yellow and red leaves that could not get off the bare branches. Again and again there would be a glorious morning followed by a pouring afternoon, and sometimes, for a week together there would be rain, nothing but rain, all day, and then the most lovely cloudless night, with the sky all out in full-blown stars...not one missing. But the little rich girl could not see much of them, for she went to bed early. The winter drew on, and she found things growing dreary. When it was too stormy to go out, and she had got tired of her toys, Nursie would take her about the house, sometimes to the housekeeper's room, where the housekeeper, who was a good, kind old woman, made much of her...sometimes to the servants' hall or the kitchen, where she was not merely a little rich girl, but absolute princess, and ran a great risk of being spoiled. Sometimes she would run off herself to the room where the bodyguards whom her father had left sat, and they showed her their arms and accoutrements, and did what they could to amuse her. Still at times she found it very dreary, and often wished that her huge great grandmother had not been a dream.

One morning the nurse left her with the housekeeper for a while. To amuse her she turned out the contents of an old cabinet upon the table. The little rich girl found her treasures, queer ancient ornaments, and many things the use of which she could not imagine, far more interesting than her own toys, and sat playing with them for two hours or more. But, at length, in handling a curious old-fashioned brooch, she ran the pin of it into her thumb, and gave a little scream with the sharpness of the pain, but would have thought little more of it had not the pain increased and her thumb begun to swell. This alarmed the housekeeper greatly. The nurse was fetched; the doctor was sent for; her hand was cared for, and long before her usual time she was put to bed. The pain still continued, and although she fell asleep and dreamed a good many dreams, there was the pain always in every dream. At last it woke her up.

The moon was shining brightly into the room. The bandage had fallen off her hand and it was burning hot. She fancied if she could hold it into the moonlight that would cool it. So she got out of bed, without waking the nurse who lay at the other end of the room, and went to the window. When she looked out she saw one of the bodyguards walking in the garden with the moonlight glancing on his gun. She was just going to tap on the window and call him, for she wanted to tell him all about it, when she bethought herself that that might wake Nursie, and she would put her into her bed again. So she resolved to go to the window of another room, and call him from there. It was so much nicer to have somebody to talk to than to lie awake in bed with the burning pain in her hand. She opened the door very gently and went through the nursery, which did not look into the garden, to go to the other window. But when she came to the foot of the old staircase there was the moon shining down from some window high up, and making the worm-eaten oak look very strange and delicate and lonely. In a moment she was putting her little feet one after the other in the silvery path up the stair, looking behind as she went, to see the shadow they made in the middle of the silver. Some little girls would have been afraid to find themselves thus alone in the middle of the night, but Tiffany was a lady.

As she went slowly up the stair, not quite sure that she was not dreaming, suddenly a great longing woke up in her heart to try once more whether she could not find the old lady with the silvery hair.

"If she is a dream," she said to herself, "then I am the likelier to find her, if I am dreaming."

So up and up she went, stair after stair, until she came to the many rooms...all just as she had seen them before. Through passage after passage she softly sped, comforting herself that if she should lose her way it would not matter much, because when she woke she would find herself in her own bed with Nursie not far off. But, as if she had known every step of the way, she walked straight to the door at the foot of the narrow stair that led to the attic.

"What if I should really find my beautiful old grandmother up there!" she said to herself as she crept up the steep steps.

When she reached the top she stood a moment listening in the dark, for there was no moon there. Yes! It was! It was the hum of the television! What a diligent grandmother to watch both day and night!

She tapped gently at the door.

"Come in, Tiffany," said the sweet voice.

The little rich girl opened the door and entered. There was the moonlight streaming in at the window, and in the middle of the moonlight sat the old lady in her black dress with the white lace, and her silvery hair mingling with the moonlight, so that you could not have told which was which.

"Come in, Tiffany," she said again. "Can you tell me what I am watching?"

"She speaks," thought Tiffany, "just as if she had seen me five minutes ago, or yesterday at the farthest...No," she answered, "I don't know what you are watching. Please I thought you were a dream. Why couldn't I find you before, Great-great-grandmother?"

"That you are hardly old enough to understand. But you would have found me sooner if you hadn't come to think I was a dream. I will give you one reason though why you couldn't find me. I didn't want you to find me."

"Why, please?"

"Because I did not want Nursie to know I was here."

"But you told me to tell Nursie."

"Yes. But I knew Nursie would not believe you. If she were to see me sitting here, she wouldn't believe me, either."

"Why?"

"Because she couldn't. She would rub her eyes, and go away and say she felt queer, and forget half of it and more, and then say it had been all a dream."

"Just like me," said Tiffany, feeling very much ashamed of herself.

"Yes, a good deal like you, but not just like you; for you've come again; and Nursie wouldn't have come again. She would have said, 'No, no'...she had had enough of such nonsense."

"Is it naughty of Nursie, then?"

"It would be naughty of you. I've never done anything for Nursie."

"And you did wash my face and hands for me," said Tiffany, beginning to cry.

The old lady smiled a sweet smile and said:

"I'm not vexed with you, my child...nor with Nursie either. But I don't want you to say anything more to Nursie about me. If she should ask you, you must just be silent. But I do not think she will ask you."

All the time they talked the old lady kept on watching the television.

"You haven't told me yet what I am watching," she said.

"Because I don't know. It's very pretty stuff."

It was indeed very pretty stuff. There were images the likes that Tiffany had never seen before. In the moonlight some shone like...what shall I say it was like? It was not white enough for silver...yes, it was like silver, but shone grey rather than white, and glittered only a little. And fine lines like thread seemed to dart now and again from the screen out towards the old lady.

"I am watching this for you, my child."

"For me! What has it to do with me, please?"

"I will tell you by and by. But first I will tell you what it is. It is soul-webs...of a particular kind. My pigeons bring it to me from over the Pacific. There is only one forest where the spiders live who make this particular kind...the finest and strongest of any. I have nearly finished my present job. What is in the set now will be enough. I have a week's work there yet, though," she added, looking at the television.

"Do you watch all day and all night, too, Great-great-great-great-grandmother?" asked the little rich girl, thinking to be very polite with so many 'greats'.

"I am not quite so great as all that," she answered, smiling almost merrily. "If you call me 'Grandmother', that will do. No, I don't work every night...only moonlit nights, and then no longer than the moon shines upon my antenna. I shan't work much longer tonight."

"And what will you do next, Grandmother?"

"Go to bed. Would you like to see my bedroom?"

"Yes, that I should."

"Then I think I won't work any longer tonight. I shall be in good time."

The old lady rose, and left her television standing just as it was. You see there was no good in putting it away, for where there was not any furniture there was no danger of being untidy.

Then she took Tiffany by the hand, but it was her bad hand and Tiffany gave a little cry of pain.

"My child!" said her grandmother, "what is the matter?"

Tiffany held her hand into the moonlight, that the old lady might see it, and told her all about it, at which she looked grave. But she only said: "Give me your other hand"; and, having led her out upon the little dark landing, opened the door on the opposite side of it. What was Tiffany's surprise to see the loveliest room she had ever seen in her life! If was large and lofty, and dome-shaped. From the center hung a lamp as round as a ball, shining as if with the brightest moonlight, which made everything visible in the room, though not so clearly that the little rich girl could tell what many of the things were. A large oval bed stood in the middle, with a coverlid of rose colour, and velvet curtains all round it of a lovely pale blue. The walls were also blue...spangled all over with what looked like stars of silver.

The old lady left her and, going to a strange-looking cabinet, opened it and took out a curious silver casket. Then she sat down on a low chair and, calling Tiffany, made her kneel before her while she looked at her hand. Having examined it, she opened the casket, and took from it a little ointment. The sweetest odour filled the room...like that of roses and lilies...as she rubbed the ointment gently all over the hot swollen hand. Her touch was so pleasant and cool that it seemed to drive away the pain and heat wherever it came.

"Oh, Grandmother! It is so nice!" said Tiffany. "Thank you; thank you."

Then the old lady went to a chest of drawers, and took out a large handkerchief of gossamer-like cambric, which she tied round her hand.

"I don't think I can let you go away tonight," she said. "Would you like to sleep with me?"

"Oh, yes, yes, dear Grandmother!" said Tiffany, and would have clapped her hands, forgetting that she could not.

"You won't be afraid, then, to go to bed with such an old woman?"

"No. You are so beautiful, Grandmother."

"But I am very old."

"And I suppose I am very young. You won't mind sleeping with such a very young woman, Grandmother?"

"You sweet little pertness!" said the old lady, and drew her towards her, and kissed her on the forehead and the cheek and the mouth.

Then she got a large silver basin, and having poured some water into it made Tiffany sit on the chair, and washed her feet. This done, she was ready for bed. And oh, what a delicious bed it was into which her grandmother laid her! She hardly could have told she was lying upon anything: she felt nothing but the softness. The old lady having undressed herself lay down beside her.

"Why don't you put out your light?" asked the little rich girl.

"That never goes out, night or day," she answered. "In the darkest night, if any of my pigeons are out on a message, they always see my moonlight and know where to fly to."

"But if somebody besides the pigeons were to see it...somebody about the house, I mean...they would come to look what it was and find you."

"The better for them, then," said the old lady. "But it does not happen above five times in a hundred years that anyone does see it. The greater part of those who do take it for a meteor, wink their eyes, and forget it again. Besides, nobody could find the room except I please. Besides, again...I will tell you a secret...if that light were to go out you would fancy yourself lying in a bare garret, on a heap of old straw, and would not see one of the pleasant things round about you all the time."

"I hope it will never go out," said the little rich girl.

"I hope not. But it is time we both went to sleep. Shall I take you in my arms?"

The little rich girl nestled close up to the old lady, who took her in both her arms and held her close to her bosom.

"Oh, dear! This is so nice!" said the little rich girl. "I didn't know anything in the world could be so comfortable. I should like to lie here forever."

"You may if you will," said the old lady. "But I must put you to one trial...not a very hard one, I hope. This night next week you must come back to me. If you don't, I do not know when you may find me again, and you will soon want me very much."

"Oh! Please, don't let me forget."

"You shall not forget. The only question is whether you will believe I am anywhere...whether you will believe I am anything but a dream. You may be sure I will do all I can to help you to come. But it will rest with yourself, after all. On the night of next Friday, you must come to me. Mind now."

"I will try," said the little rich girl.

"Then good night," said the old lady, and kissed the forehead which lay in her bosom.

In a moment more the little rich girl was dreaming in the midst of the loveliest dreams...of summer seas and moonlight and mossy springs and great murmuring trees, and beds of wild flowers with such odours as she had never smelled before. But, after all, no dream could be more lovely than what she had left behind when she fell asleep.

In the morning she found herself in her own bed. There was no handkerchief or anything else on her hand, only a sweet odour lingered about it. The swelling had all gone down; the prick of the brooch had vanished...in fact, her hand was perfectly well.

Chapter 12

Jonny spent many nights in the garage. His father and he had taken Mrs. Mo into the secret, for they knew Mother could hold her tongue, which was more than could be said of all wives. But Jonny did not tell her that every night he spent in the garage, part of it went in earning a new coat for her.

Mrs. Mo was such a nice good mother! All mothers are nice and good more or less, but Mrs. Mo was nice and good all more and no less. She made and kept a little heaven in that poor apartment on the high hillside...for her husband and son to go home to out of the low and rather dreary garage in which they worked. I doubt if the little rich girl was very much happier even in the arms of her huge great-grandmother than Earl and Jonny were in the arms of Mrs. Mo. True, her hands were hard and chapped and large, but it was with work for them; and therefore, in the sight of those with understanding, her hands were so much the more beautiful. And if Jonny worked hard to get her a coat, she worked hard every day to get him comforts which he would have missed much more than she would a new coat even in winter. Not that she and Jonny ever thought of how much they worked for each other: that would have spoiled everything.

When left alone in the garage Jonny always worked on for an hour or two at first, cleaning the cars, listening to news of the PG&E tunnel which, according to Wrecker, would lead at last into the deserted storage area. After that, he would set out on a reconnoitering expedition. In order to manage this, or rather the return from it, better than the first time, he had bought a huge ball of fine string, having learned the trick from an old Greek legend, whose history his mother had often told him. Not that the Greeks had ever used a ball of string...I should be sorry to be supposed so far out in my classics...but the principle was the same as that used against the bull-beast in one of the stories. The end of this string he fastened to the door at the bottom of the old stairway, which figured as a good anchor, and then, with the ball in his hand, unrolling it as he went, set out in the dark through the tunnels of the lowlifes' territory. The first night or two he came upon nothing worth remembering; saw only a little of the home-life of the lowlifes in the various caves and chambers they called houses; failed in coming upon anything to cast light upon the foregoing design which kept the inundation for the present in the background. But at length, I think on the third or fourth night, he found, partly guided by the noise of their implements, a company of evidently the best miners amongst them, hard at work. What were they about? It could not well be the inundation, seeing that had in the meantime been postponed to something else. Then what was it? He lurked and watched, every now and then in the greatest risk of being detected, but without success. He had again and again to retreat in haste; proceeding rendered the more difficult that he had to gather up his string as he returned upon its course. It was not that he was afraid of the lowlifes, but that he was afraid of their finding out that they were watched, which might have prevented the discovery at which he aimed. Sometimes his haste had to be such that, when he reached home towards morning, his string, for lack of time to wind it up as he "lost the lowlifes," would be in what seemed a most hopeless entanglement; but after a good sleep, though a short one, he always found his mother had got it right again. There it was, wound in a most remarkable ball, ready for use the moment he should want it!

"I can't think how you do it, Mother," he would say.

"I follow the thread," she would answer "…just as you do in the tunnels."

She never had more to say about it; but the less clever she was with her words, the more clever she was with her hands; and the less his mother said, the more Jonny believed she had to say.

But still he had made no discovery as to what the lowlife miners were up to.

Chapter 13

About this time the gentlemen whom the rich man had left behind him to watch over the little rich girl each had occasion to doubt the testimony of his own eyes, for more than strange were the objects to which they would bear witness. They were of one sort...creatures...but so grotesque and misshapen as to be more like a child's drawings or paintings than anything natural. They saw them only at night, while on guard about the house. The testimony of the man who first reported having seen one of them was that, as he was walking slowly round the house, while yet in the shadow, he caught sight of a creature standing on its hind legs in the moonlight, with its forefeet upon a window ledge, staring in at the window. Its body might have been that of a dog or wolf, he thought, but he declared on his honour that its head was twice the size it ought to have been for the size of its body, and as round as a ball, while the face, which it turned upon him as it fled, was more like one carved by a boy upon the pumpkin inside which he is going to put a candle than anything else he could think of. It rushed into the garden. He shot at it, and thought he must have struck it; for it gave an unearthly howl, but he could not find the beast even though he searched all about the place where it vanished. They laughed at him until he was driven to hold his tongue, and said he must have taken too long a pull at the scotch flask. But before two nights were over he had one to side with him, for he, too, had seen something strange, only quite different from that reported by the other. The description the second man gave of the creature he had seen was yet more grotesque and unlikely. They were both laughed at by the rest; but night after night another came over to their side, until at last there was only one left to laugh at all his companions. Two nights more passed, and he saw nothing; but on the third he came rushing from the garden to the other two before the house, in such an agitation that they declared...for it was their turn now...that the hair on his head was standing up. Running with him into that part of the garden which I have already described, they saw a score of creatures, to not one of which they could give a name, and not one of which was like another, hideous and ludicrous at once, gamboling on the lawn in the moonlight. The supernatural or rather subnatural ugliness of their faces, the length of legs and necks in some, the apparent absence of both or either in others, made the spectators, although in one consent as to what they saw, yet doubtful, as I have said, of the evidence of their own eyes...and ears as well; for the noises they made, although not loud, were as uncouth and varied as their forms, and could be described neither as grunts nor squeaks nor roars nor howls nor barks nor yells nor screams nor croaks nor hisses nor mews nor shrieks, but only as something like all of them mingled in one horrible dissonance. Keeping in the shade, the watchers had a few moments to recover themselves before the hideous assembly suspected their presence; but all at once, as if by common consent, they scampered off in the direction of a great false rock, and vanished before the men had come to themselves sufficiently to think of following them.

My readers will suspect what there were; but I will now give them full information concerning them. They were, of course, household animals belonging to the lowlifes, whose ancestors had taken their ancestors years before from the upper regions of light into the lower regions of darkness. The original stocks of these horrible creatures were very much the same as the animals now seen about the city and homes, with the exception of a few of them, which had been creatures such as chimps. But in the course of time all had undergone even greater changes than had passed upon their owners. They had altered...that is, their descendants had altered...into such creatures as I have not attempted to describe except in the vaguest manner...the various parts of their bodies assuming, in an apparently arbitrary and self-willed manner, the most abnormal developments. Indeed, so little did any distinct type predominate in some of the bewildering results, that you could only have guessed at any known animal as the original, and even then, what likeness remained would be more one of general expression than of definable conformation. But what increased the gruesomeness tenfold was that, from constant domestic, or indeed rather family association with the lowlifes, their countenances had grown in grotesque resemblance to the human. No one understands animals who does not see that every one of them, even amongst the fishes, it may be with a dimness and vagueness infinitely remote, yet shadows the human: in the case of these the human resemblance had greatly increased: while their owners had sunk towards them, they had risen towards their owners. But the conditions of subterranean life being equally unnatural for both, while the lowlifes were worse, the creatures had not improved by the approximation, and its result would have appeared far more ludicrous than consoling to the warmest lover of animal nature. I shall now explain how it was that just then these animals began to show themselves about the rich man's house.

The lowlifes, as Jonny had discovered, were mining on...at work both day and night, in divisions, urging the scheme after which he lay in wait. In the course of their tunneling they had broken into the channel of a small sewer, but the break being in the top of it, no water had escaped to interfere with their work. Some of the creatures, hovering as they often did about their masters, had found the hole, and had, with the curiosity which had grown to a passion from the restraints of their unnatural circumstances, proceeded to explore the channel. The sewer was the same which ran under the rich man's house, and had an opening by the little stream which ran out by the seat on which Tiffany and her father had sat as I have told, and the lowlife creatures found it jolly fun to get out for a romp on a smooth lawn such as they had never seen in all their poor miserable lives. But although they had partaken enough of the nature of their owners to delight in annoying and alarming any of the people whom they met in the city, they were, of course, incapable of designs of their own, or of intentionally furthering those of their masters.

For several nights after, the bodyguards were at length of one mind as to the fact of the visits of some horrible creatures, whether bodily or spectral they could not yet say, they watched with special attention that part of the garden where they had last seen them. Perhaps indeed they gave in consequence too little attention to the house. But the creatures were too cunning to be easily caught; nor were the watchers quick-eyed enough to descry the head, or the keen eyes in it, which, from the opening whence the stream and garden drained, would watch them in turn, ready, the moment they should leave the lawn, to report the place clear.

Chapter 14

During the whole of the week Tiffany had been thinking every other moment of her promise to the old lady, although even now she could not feel quite sure that she had not been dreaming. Could it really be that an old lady lived up in the top of the house, with pigeons and a strange television, and a lamp that never went out? She was, however, none the less determined, on the coming Friday, to ascend the three stairs, walk through the passages with the many doors, and try to find the attic in which she had either seen or dreamed her grandmother.

Her nurse could not help wondering what had come to the child...she would sit so thoughtfully silent, and even in the midst of a game with her would so suddenly fall into a dreamy mood. But Tiffany took care to betray nothing, whatever efforts Nursie might make to get at her thoughts. And Nursie had to say to herself: "What an odd child she is!" and give up.

At length the longed-for Friday arrived, and lest Nursie should be moved to watch her, Tiffany endeavoured to keep herself as quiet as possible. In the afternoon she asked for her doll's house, and went on arranging and rearranging the various rooms and their inhabitants for a whole hour. Then she gave a sigh and threw herself back in her chair. One of the dolls would not sit, and another would not stand, and they were all very tiresome. Indeed, there was one would not even lie down, which was too bad. But it was now getting dark, and the darker it got the more excited Tiffany became, and the more she felt it necessary to be composed.

"I see you want your tea, young lady," said the nurse: "I will go and get it. The room feels close: I will open the window a little. The evening is mild: it won't hurt you."

"There's no fear of that, Nursie," said Tiffany, wishing she had put off going for the tea till it was darker, when she might have made her attempt with every advantage.

I fancy Nursie was longer in returning than she had intended; for when Tiffany, who had been lost in thought, looked up, she saw it was nearly dark, and at the same moment caught sight of a pair of eyes, bright with a green light, glowering at her through the open window. The next instant something leaped into the room. It was like a cat, with legs as long as a horse's, Tiffany said, but its body no bigger and its legs no thicker than those of a cat. She was too frightened to cry out, but not too frightened to jump from her chair and run from the room.

It is plain enough to every one of my readers what she ought to have done...and indeed Tiffany thought of it herself; but when she came to the foot of the old stair, just outside the nursery door, she imagined the creature running up those long ascents after her, and pursuing her through the dark passages...which, after all, might lead to no attic! That thought was too much. Her heart failed her, and turning from the stair, she rushed along to the hall, whence, finding the front door open, she darted into the court pursued...at least she thought so...by the creature. No one happening to see her, on she ran, unable to think for fear, and ready to run anywhere to elude the awful creature with the stilt-legs. Not daring to look behind her, she rushed straight out of the gate and up the hill. It was foolish indeed...thus to run farther and farther from all who could help her, as if she had been seeking a fit spot for the lowlife creature to eat her in at his leisure; but that is the way fear serves us: it always sides with the thing we are afraid of.

The little rich girl was soon out of breath with running uphill; but she ran on, for she fancied the horrible creature just behind her, forgetting that, had it been after her, such long legs as those must have overtaken her long ago. At last she could run no longer, and fell, unable even to scream, by the roadside, where she lay for some time half-dead with terror. But finding nothing lay hold of her, and her breath beginning to come back, she ventured at length to get half up and peer anxiously about her. It was now so dark she could see nothing. Not a single star was out. She could not even tell in what direction the house lay, and between her and home she fancied the dreadful creature lying ready to pounce upon her. She saw now that she ought to have run up the stairs at once. It was well she did not scream; for, although very few of the lowlifes had come out for weeks, a stray idler or two might have heard her. She sat down upon a curb and nobody but one who had done something wrong could have been more miserable. She had quite forgotten her promise to visit her grandmother. A raindrop fell on her face. She looked up, and for a moment her terror was lost in astonishment. At first she thought the rising moon had left her place, and drawn nigh to see what could be the matter with the little girl, sitting alone, without hat or cloak, on the dark bare mountain; but she soon saw she was mistaken, for there was no light on the ground at her feet, and no shadow anywhere. But a great silvery globe was hanging in the air; and as she gazed at the lovely thing, her courage revived. If she were but indoors again, she would fear nothing, not even the terrible creature with the long legs! But how was she to find her way back? What could the light be? Could it be…? No, it couldn't. But what if it should be…yes…it must be…her great-great-grandmother's lamp, which guided her pigeons home through the darkest night! She jumped up: she had but to keep that light in view and she must find the house. It was brighter than even the mist-shrouded street lamps!

Her heart grew strong. Speedily, yet softly, she walked down the hill, hoping to pass the watching creature unseen. Dark as it was, there was little danger now of choosing the wrong road. And…which was most strange…the light that filled her eyes from the lamp, instead of blinding them for a moment to the object upon which they next fell, enabled her for a moment to see it, despite the darkness. By looking at the lamp and then dropping her eyes, she could see the road for a yard or two in front of her, and this saved her from several falls, for the road was very rough. But all at once, to her dismay, it vanished, and the terror of the beast, which had left her the moment she began to return, again laid hold of her heart. The same instant, however, she caught the light of the windows, and knew exactly where she was. It was too dark to run, but she made what haste she could, and reached the gate in safety. She found the house door still open, ran through the hall, and without even looking into the nursery, bounded straight up the stair, and the next, and the next: then turning to the right, ran through the long avenue of silent rooms, and found her way at once to the door at the foot of the attic stair.

When first the nurse missed her, she fancied she was playing her a trick, and for some time took no trouble about her; but at last, getting frightened, she had begun to search; and when the little rich girl entered, the whole household was hither and thither over the house, hunting for her. A few seconds after she reached the stair of the attic they had even begun to search the neglected rooms, in which they would never have thought of looking had they not already searched every other place they could think of in vain. But by this time she was knocking at the old lady's door.

Chapter 15

"Come in, Tiffany," said the silvery voice of her grandmother.

The little rich girl opened the door and peeped in. But the room was quite dark and there was no sound of the television. She grew frightened once more, thinking that, although the room was there, the old lady might be a dream after all. Every little girl knows how dreadful it is to find a room empty where she thought somebody was; but Tiffany had to fancy for a moment that the person she came to find was nowhere at all. She remembered, however, that at night she watched only in the moonlight, and concluded that must be why there was no sweet, bee-like humming: the old lady might be somewhere in the darkness. Before she had time to think another thought, she heard her voice again, saying as before:

"Come in, Tiffany."

From the sound, she understood at once that she was not in the room beside her. Perhaps she was in her bedroom. She turned across the passage, feeling her way to the other door. When her hand fell on the lock, again the old lady spoke:

"Shut the other door behind you, Tiffany. I always close the door of my workroom when I go to my chamber."

Tiffany wondered to hear her voice so plainly through the door: having shut the other, she opened it and went in. Oh, what a lovely haven to reach from the darkness and fear through which she had come! The soft light made her feel as if she were going into the heart of the milkiest pearl; while the blue walls and their silver start for a moment perplexed her with the fancy that they were in reality the sky which she had left outside a minute ago covered with rainclouds.

"I've lighted a fire for you, Tiffany: you're cold and wet," said her grandmother.

Then Tiffany looked again, and saw that what she had taken for a huge bouquet of red roses on a low stand against the wall was in fact a fire which burned in the shapes of the loveliest and reddest roses, glowing gorgeously between the heads and wings of two cherubs of shining silver. And when she came nearer, she found that the smell of roses with which the room was filled came from the fire-roses on the hearth. Her grandmother was dressed in the loveliest pale blue velvet, over which her hair, no longer white, but of rich golden color, streamed like a cataract, here falling in full gathered heaps, there rushing away in smooth shining falls. And ever as she looked, the hair seemed pouring down from her head and vanishing in a golden mist ere it reached the floor. It flowed from under the edge of a circle of shining silver, set with alternated pearls and opals. On her dress was no ornament whatever, neither was there a ring on her hand, or a necklace or carcanet about her neck. But her slippers glimmered with the light of the Milky Way, for they were covered with seed pearls and opals in one mass. Her face was that of a woman only twenty-three.

The little rich girl was so bewildered with astonishment and admiration that she could hardly thank her, and drew quiet with timidity, feeling dirty and uncomfortable. The lady was seated on a low chair by the side of the fire, with hands outstretched to take her, but the little rich girl hung back with a troubled smile.

"Why, what's the matter?" asked her grandmother. "You haven't been doing anything wrong...I know that by your face, though it is rather miserable. What's the matter, my dear?"

And she still held out her arms.

"Dear Grandmother," said Tiffany, "I'm not so sure that I haven't done something wrong. I ought to have run up to you at once when the long-legged cat-thing came in at the window, instead of running out on the city streets and making myself such a fright."

"You were taken by surprise, my child, and are not so likely to do it again. It is when people do wrong things willfully that they are the more likely to do them again. Come."

And still she held out her arms.

"But Grandmother, you're so beautiful and grand! And I am so dirty with mud and rain!...I should quite spoil your beautiful blue dress."

With a merry little laugh the lady sprung from her chair, more lightly far than Tiffany herself could, caught the child to her bosom, and, kissing the tearstained face over and over, sat down with her in her lap.

"Oh, Grandmother! You'll make yourself such a mess!" cried Tiffany, clinging to her.

"You darling! Do you think I care more for my dress than for my little girl? Besides...look here."

As she spoke she set her down, and Tiffany saw to her dismay that the lovely dress was covered with the mud of her fall on the city street. But the lady stooped to the fire, and taking from it, by the stalk in her fingers, one of the burning roses, passed it once and again and a third time over the front of her dress; and when Tiffany looked, not a single stain was to be discovered.

"There!" said her grandmother. "You won't mind coming to me now?"

But Tiffany again hung back, eyeing the flaming rose which the lady held in her hand.

"You're not afraid of the rose...are you?" she said, about to throw it on the hearth again.

"Oh! Don't please!" cried Tiffany. "Won't you hold it to my frock and my hands and my face? And I'm afraid my feet and my knees want it too!"

"No," answered her grandmother, smiling a little sadly, as she threw the rose from her; "it is too hot for you yet. It would set your frock in a flame. Besides, I don't want to make you clean tonight. I want your nurse and the rest of the people to see you as you are, for you will have to tell them how you ran away for fear of the long-legged cat-thing. I should like to wash you, but they would not believe you then. Do you see that bath behind you?"

The little rich girl looked, and saw a large oval tub of silver, shining brilliantly in the light of the wonderful lamp.

"Go and look into it," said the lady.

Tiffany went, and came back very silent with her eyes shining.

"What did you see?" asked her grandmother.

"The sky and the moon and the stars," she answered. "It looked as if there was no bottom to it."

The lady smiled a pleased satisfied smile, and was silent also for a few moments. Then she said:

"Any time you want a bath, come to me. I know you have a bath every morning, but sometimes you want one at night, too."

"Thank you, Grandmother; I will...I will indeed," answered Tiffany, and was again silent for some moments thinking. Then she said: "How was it, Grandmother, that I saw your beautiful lamp...not the light of it only...but the great round silvery lamp itself, hanging alone in the great open air, high up? It was your lamp I saw...wasn't it?"

"Yes, my child; it was my lamp."

"Then how was it? I don't see a window all round."

"When I please I can make the lamp shine through the walls...shine so strong that it melts them away from before the sight, and shows itself as you saw it. But, as I told you, it is not everybody who can see it."

"How is it that I can, then? I'm sure I don't know."

"It is a gift born with you. And one day I hope everybody will have it."

"But how do you make it shine through the walls?"

"Ah! That you would not understand if I were to try ever so much to make you...not yet...not yet. But," added the lady, rising, "you must sit in my chair while I get you the present I have been preparing for you. I told you my watching was for you. It is finished now, and I am going to fetch the result. I have been keeping it warm under one of my brooding pigeons."

Tiffany sat down in the low chair, and her grandmother left her, shutting the door behind her. The child sat gazing, now at the rose fire, now at the starry walls, now at the silver light; and a great quietness grew in her heart. If all the long-legged cat-things in the world had come rushing at her then she would not have been afraid of them for a moment. How this was she could not tell...she only knew there was no fear in her, and everything was so right and safe that it could not get in.

She had been gazing at the lovely lamp for some minutes fixedly; turning her eyes, she found the wall had vanished, for she was looking out on the dark cloudy night. But though she heard the wind blowing, none of it blew upon her. In a moment more the clouds themselves parted, or rather vanished like the wall, and she looked straight into the starry herds, flashing gloriously in the dark blue.

It was but for a moment. The clouds gathered again and shut out the stars; the wall gathered again and shut out the clouds; and there stood the lady beside her with the loveliest smile on her face, and a shimmering ball in her hand, about the size of a pigeon's egg.

"There, Tiffany; there is my work for you!" she said, holding out the ball to the little rich girl.

She took it in her hand, and looked at it all over. It sparkled a little, and shone here and there, but not much. It was of a sort of grey-whiteness, something like spun glass.

"Is this all your work, Grandmother?" she asked.

"All since you came to the house. There is more there than you think."

"How pretty it is! What am I to do with it, please?"

"That I will now explain to you," answered the lady, turning from her and going to her cabinet.

She came back with a small ring in her hand. Then she took the ball from Tiffany, and did something with the two...Tiffany could not tell what.

"Give me your hand," she said.

Tiffany held up her right hand.

"Yes, that is the hand I want," said the lady, and put the ring on the forefinger of it.

"What a beautiful ring!" said Tiffany. "What is the stone called?"

"It is a fire-opal."

"Please, am I to keep it?"

"Always."

"Oh, thank you, Grandmother! It's prettier than anything I ever saw, except those...of all colors...in your...Please, is that a real crown on your head?"

"Yes, it is my crown. The stone in your ring is of the same sort...only not so good. It has only red, but mine have all colors, you see."

"Yes, Grandmother. I will take such care of it! But..." she added, hesitating.

"But what?" asked her grandmother.

"What am I to say when Nursie asks me where I got it?"

"You will ask her where you got it," answered the lady smiling.

"I don't see how I can do that."

"You will, though."

"Of course I will, if you say so. But, you know, I can't pretend not to know."

"Of course not. But don't trouble yourself about it. You will see when the time comes."

So saying, the lady turned, and threw the little ball into the rose fire.

"Oh, Grandmother!" exclaimed Tiffany; "I thought you had made it for me."

"So I did, my child. And you've got it."

"No; it's burnt in the fire!"

The lady put her hand in the fire, brought out the ball, glimmering as before, and held it towards her. Tiffany stretched out her hand to take it, but the lady turned and, going to her cabinet, opened a drawer, and laid the ball in it.

"Have I done anything to vex you, Grandmother?" asked Tiffany pitifully.

"No, my darling. But you must understand that no one ever gives anything to another properly and really without keeping it. That ball is yours."

"Oh! I'm not to take it with me! You are going to keep it for me!"

"You are to take it with you. I've fastened the end of it to the ring on your finger."

Tiffany looked at the ring.

"I can't see it there, Grandmother," she said.

"Feel...a little way from the ring...towards the cabinet," said the lady.

"Oh! I do feel it!" exclaimed the rich girl. "But I can't see it," she added, looking close to her outstretched hand.

"No. The thread is too fine for you to see it. You can only feel it. Now you can fancy how much work that took, although it does seem such a little ball."

"But what use can I make of it, if it lies in your cabinet?"

"That is what I will explain to you. It would be of no use to you...it wouldn't be yours at all if it did not lie in my cabinet. Now listen. If ever you find yourself in any danger...such, for example, as you were in this evening...you must take off your ring and put it under the pillow of your bed. Then you must lay your forefinger, the same that wore the ring, upon the thread, and follow the thread wherever it leads you."

"Oh, how delightful! It will lead me to you, Grandmother, I know!"

"Yes. But, remember, it may seem to you a very roundabout way indeed, and you must not doubt the thread. Of one thing you may be sure, that while you hold it, I hold it too."

"It is very wonderful!" said Tiffany thoughtfully. Then suddenly, becoming aware, she jumped up, crying: "Oh, Grandmother! Here have I been sitting all this time in your chair, and you standing! I beg your pardon."

The lady laid her hand on her shoulder, and said:

"Sit down again, Tiffany. Nothing pleases me better than to see anyone sit in my chair. I am only too glad to stand so long as anyone will sit in it."

"How kind of you!" said the little rich girl, and sat down again.

"It makes me happy," said the lady.

"But," said Tiffany, still puzzled, "won't the thread get in somebody's way and be broken, if the one end is fast to my ring, and the other laid in your cabinet?"

"You will find all that arranges itself. I am afraid it is time for you to go."

"Mightn't I stay and sleep with you tonight, Grandmother?"

"No, not tonight. If I had meant for you to stay tonight, I should have given you a bath; but you know everybody in the house is miserable about you, and it would be cruel to keep them so all night. You must go downstairs."

"I'm so glad, Grandmother, you didn't say 'Go home,' for this is my home. May I not call this my home?"

"You may, my child. And I trust you will always think it your home. Now come. I must take you back without anyone seeing you."

"Please, I want to ask you one question more," said Tiffany. "Is it because you have your crown on that you look so young?"

"No, child," answered her grandmother; "it is because I felt so young this evening that I put my crown on. And I thought you would like to see your old grandmother in her best."

"Why do you call yourself old? You're not old, Grandmother."

"I am very old indeed. It is so silly of people...I don't mean you, for you are such a tiny, and couldn't know better...but it is so silly of people to fancy that old age means crookedness and witheredness and feebleness and sticks and spectacles and rheumatism and forgetfulness! It is so silly! Old age has nothing whatever to do with all that. The right old age means strength and beauty and mirth and courage and clear eyes and strong painless limbs. I am older than you are able to think, and..."

"And look at you, Grandmother!" cried Tiffany, jumping up and flinging her arms about her neck. "I won't be so silly again, I promise you. At least...I'm rather afraid to promise...but if I am, I promise to be sorry for it...I do. I wish I were as old as you, Grandmother. I don't think you are ever afraid of anything."

"Not for long, at least, my child. Perhaps by the time I am two thousand years of age, I shall, indeed, never be afraid of anything. But I confess I have sometimes been afraid about my children...sometimes about you, Tiffany."

"Oh, I'm so sorry, Grandmother! Tonight, I suppose, you mean."

"Yes...a little tonight; but a good deal when you had all but made up your mind that I was a dream, and no real great-great-grandmother. You must not suppose I am blaming you for that. I dare say you could not help it."

"I don't know, Grandmother," said the little rich girl, beginning to cry. "I can't always do myself as I should like. And I don't always try. I'm very sorry anyhow."

The lady stooped, lifted her in her arms, and sat down with her in her chair, holding her close to her bosom. In a few minutes the little rich girl had sobbed herself to sleep. How long she slept, I do not know. When she came to herself she was sitting in her own high chair at the nursery table, with her doll's house before her.

Chapter 16

The same moment her nurse came into the room, sobbing. When she saw her sitting there she started back with a loud cry of amazement and joy. Then running to her, she caught her in her arms and covered her with kisses.

"My precious darling little girl! Where have you been? What has happened to you? We've all been crying our eyes out, and searching the house from top to bottom for you."

"Not quite from the top," thought Tiffany to herself; and she might have added, "not quite to the bottom," perhaps, if she had known all. But the one she would not, and the other she could not say.

"Oh, Nursie! I've had such a dreadful adventure!" she replied, and told her all about the cat-thing with the long legs, and how she ran out upon the city streets, and came back again. But she said nothing of her grandmother or her lamp.

"And there we've been searching for you all over the house for more than an hour and a half!" exclaimed the nurse. "But that's no matter, now we've got you! Only, young lady, I must say," she added, her mood changing, "what you ought to have done was to call for your own Nursie to come and help you, instead of running out of the house, and up the hill, in that wild, I must say, foolish fashion."

"Well, Nursie," said Tiffany quietly, "perhaps if you had a big cat, all legs, running at you, you mightn't exactly know what was the wisest thing to do at the moment."

"I wouldn't run up the hill, anyhow," returned Nursie.

"Not if you had time to think about it. But when those creatures came at you that night on the hill, you were so frightened yourself that you lost your way home."

This put a stop to Nursie's reproaches. She had been on the point of saying that the long-legged cat-thing must have been a twilight fancy of the little rich girl's, but the memory of the horrors of that night, and of the talking-to which the rich father had given her in consequence, prevented her from saying what after all she did not half believe...having a strong suspicion that the cat-thing was a lowlife; for she knew nothing of the difference between the lowlifes and their creatures: she counted them all just lowlifes.

Without another word she went and got some fresh tea and bread and butter for the little rich girl. Before she returned, the whole household, headed by the housekeeper, burst into the nursery to exult over their darling. The bodyguards followed, and were ready enough to believe all she told them about the long-legged cat-thing. Indeed, though wise enough to say nothing about it, they remembered, with no little horror, just such a creature amongst those they had surprised at their gambols upon the little rich girl's lawn. In their own hearts they blamed themselves for not having kept better watch. And their leader gave orders that from this night the front door and all the windows on the ground floor should be locked immediately as the sun set, and opened after upon no pretense whatever. The bodyguards redoubled their vigilance, and for some time there was no further cause of alarm.

When the little rich girl woke the next morning, her nurse was bending over her.

"How your ring does glow this morning, dear girl! Just like a fiery rose!" she said.

"Does it, Nursie?" returned Tiffany. "Who gave me the ring, Nursie? I know I've had it a long time, but where did I get it? I don't remember."

"I think it must have been your mother gave it to you, little one; but really, for as long as you have worn it, I don't remember that ever I heard," answered her nurse.

"I will ask my papa the next time he comes," said Tiffany.

Chapter 17

The spring so dear to all creatures, young and old, came at last, and before the first few days of it had gone, the rich man came through its budding parks to see his little daughter. He had been in a distant part of the world all the winter, for he was not in the habit of stopping in one great city or of visiting only his favourite country houses, but he moved from place to place, that all his businesses might know him. Wherever he journeyed, he kept a constant lookout for the ablest and best people to put into office; and wherever he found himself mistaken, and those he had appointed incapable or unjust, he removed them at once. Hence you see it was his care of the people that kept him from seeing his daughter so often as he would have liked. You may wonder why he did not take her about with him; but there were several reasons against his doing so, and I suspect her great-great-grandmother had had a principal hand in preventing it. Once more Tiffany heard as he drove up in his great white car.

After they had been alone for a little while, she thought of what she had resolved to ask him.

"Please, Papa," she said, "will you tell me where I got this pretty ring? I can't remember."

The rich man looked at it. A strange beautiful smile spread like sunshine over his face, and an answering smile, but at the same time a questioning one, spread like moonlight over Tiffany's.

"It was your mother's once," he said.

"And why isn't it hers now?" asked Tiffany.

"She does not want it now," said the rich man, looking grave.

"Why doesn't she want it now?"

"Because she's gone where all those rings are made."

"And when shall I see her?" asked the little rich girl.

"Not for some time yet," answered the rich man, and the tears came into his eyes.

Tiffany did not remember her mother and did not know why her father looked so, and why the tears came in his eyes; but she put her arms round his neck and kissed him, and asked no more questions.

The rich man was much disturbed on hearing the report of the bodyguards concerning the creatures they had seen; and I presume would have taken Tiffany with him that very day, but for what the presence of the ring on her finger assured him of. About an hour before he left, Tiffany saw him go up the old stair; and he did not come down again till they were just ready to start; and she thought with herself that he had been up to see the old lady. When he went away he left another six gentlemen behind him, that there might be a full six of them always on guard.

And now, in the lovely spring weather, Tiffany was out in the garden and city the greater part of the day. In the warmer hollows there were lovely flower shops with lovely primroses, and not so many that she ever got tired of them. As often as she saw a new one opening an eye of light in the blind earth, she would clap her hands with gladness, and unlike some children I know, instead of pulling it, would touch it as tenderly as if it had been a new baby, and, having made its acquaintance, would leave it as happy as she found it. She treated the plants on which they grew like birds' nests in the park; every fresh flower was like a new little bird to her. She would pay visits to all the flower-nests she knew, remembering each by itself. She would go down on her hands and knees beside each one and say: "Good morning! Are you all smelling very sweet this morning? Good-bye!" and then she would go to another nest, and say the same. It was a favourite amusement with her. There were many flowers up and down the hills in shops and flower boxes and parks, and she loved them all, but the primroses were her favourites.

"They're not too shy, and they're not a bit forward," she would say to Nursie.

There were dogs and cats about, over the city, and when the little pups and kittens came she was as pleased with them as with the flowers. The dogs and cats belonged to the apartment and condo people mostly...a few of them to Jonny's mother; but there were a good many wild ones that seemed to belong to nobody. These the lowlifes counted theirs, and it was upon them partly that they lived. They set snares and dug pits for them; and did not scruple to take what tame ones happened to be caught; but they did not try to steal them in any other manner, because they were afraid of many of the dogs the city-people kept to watch them, for the knowing dogs always tried to bite their feet. But the lowlifes had a kind of sheep of their own...very queer creatures, which they drove out to feed at night, and the other lowlife creatures were wise enough to keep good watch over them, for they knew they should have their bones by and by.

Chapter 18

Jonny was as watchful as ever, but was almost getting tired of his ill success. Every other night or so he followed the lowlifes about, as they went on digging and boring, and getting as near them as he could, watched them from behind stones and rocks; but as yet he seemed no nearer finding out what they had in view. As at first, he always kept hold of the end of his string, while he found some heavy object, left just outside the hole by which he entered the lowlifes' country from the garage, to serve as an anchor and hold fast the other end. The lowlifes, hearing no more noise in that quarter, had ceased to apprehend an immediate invasion, and kept no watch.

One night, after dodging about and listening till he was nearly falling asleep with weariness, he began to roll up his ball, for he had resolved to go home to bed. It was not long, however, before he began to feel bewildered. One after another he passed lowlife houses, caves, that is, occupied by lowlife families, and at length was sure they were many more than he had passed as he came. He had to use great caution to pass unseen...they lay so close together. Could his string have led him wrong? He still followed winding it, and still it led him into more thickly populated quarters, until he became quite uneasy, and indeed apprehensive; for although he was not afraid of the lowlifes, he was afraid of not finding his way out. But what could he do? It was of no use to sit down and wait for the morning...the morning made no difference here. It was dark, and always dark; and if his string failed him he was helpless. He might even arrive within a yard of the garage and never know it. Seeing he could do nothing better he would at least find where the end of his string was, and, if possible, how it had come to play him such a trick. He knew by the size of the ball that he was getting pretty near the last of it, when he began to feel a tugging and pulling at it. What could it mean? Turning a sharp corner, he thought he heard strange sounds. These grew, as he went on, to a scuffling and growling and squeaking; and the noise increased, until, turning a second sharp corner, he found himself in the midst of it, and the same moment tumbled over a wallowing mass, which he knew must be a knot of the lowlifes' creatures. Before he could recover his feet, he had caught some great scratches on his face and several severe bites on his legs and arms. But as he scrambled to get up, his hand fell upon the PG&E pickaxe that he had used as an anchor that night, and before the horrid beasts could do him any serious harm, he was laying about with it right and left in the dark. The hideous cries which followed gave him the satisfaction of knowing that he had punished some of them pretty smartly for their rudeness, and by their scampering and their retreating howls, he perceived that he had routed them. He stood for a little, weighing his battle-axe in his hand as if it had been the most precious lump of metal...but indeed no lump of gold itself could have been so precious at the time as that common tool...then untied the end of the string from it, put the ball in his pocket, and still stood thinking. It was clear that the lowlifes' creatures had found the pickaxe, had between them carried it off, and had so led him he knew not where. But for all his thinking he could not tell what he ought to do, until suddenly he became aware of a glimmer of light in the distance. Without a moment's hesitation he set out for it, as fast as the unknown and rugged way would permit. Yet again turning a corner, led by the dim light, he spied something quite new in his experience of the underground regions...a small irregular shape of something shining. Going up to it, he found it was a piece of mica, or Muscovy glass, called sheep-silver in Scotland, and the light flickered as if from a fire behind it. After trying in vain for some time to discover an entrance to the place where it was burning, he came at length to a small chamber in which an opening, high in the wall, revealed a glow beyond. To this opening he managed to scramble up, and then he saw a strange sight.

Below sat a little group of lowlifes around a fire, the smoke of which vanished in the darkness far aloft. The sides of the cave were full of shining glass and minerals like those of the palace hall; and the company was evidently of a superior order, for every one wore stones and trinkets about head, or arms, or waist, shining gorgeous colours in the light of the fire. Nor had Jonny looked long before he recognized the king himself, and found that he had made his way into the inner apartment of the royal family. He had never had such a good chance of hearing something! He crept through the hole as softly as he could, scrambled a good way down the wall towards them without attracting attention, and then sat down and listened. The king, evidently the queen, and probably the crown prince and the being that he would later realize was the Prime Minister were talking together. He was sure of the queen by her shoes, for as she warmed her feet at the fire, he saw them quite plainly.

"That will be fun!" said the one he took for the crown prince.

It was the first whole sentence he heard.

"I don't see why you should think it such a grand affair!" said his stepmother, tossing her head backward.

"You must remember, my spouse," interposed His Majesty, as if making excuse for his son, "he has got the same blood in him. His mother..."

"Don't talk to me of his mother! You positively encourage his unnatural fancies. Whatever belongs to that mother ought to be cut out of him."

"You forget yourself, my dear!" said the king.

"I don't," said the queen, "nor you either. If you expect me to approve of such coarse tastes, you will find yourself mistaken. I don't wear shoes for nothing."

"You must acknowledge, however," the king said, with a little groan, "that this at least is no whim of Noears, but a matter of State policy. You are well aware that his gratification comes purely from the pleasure of sacrificing himself to the public good. Does it not, Noears?"

"Yes, Father; of course it does. Only it will be nice to make her cry. I'll have the skin taken off between her toes, and tie them up till they grow together. Then her feet will be like other people's, and there will be no occasion for her to wear shoes."

"Do you mean to insinuate I've got toes, you unnatural wretch?" cried the queen; and she moved angrily towards Noears. The councillor, however, who was betwixt them, leaned forward so as to prevent her touching him, but only as if to address the prince.

"Your Royal Highness," he said, "possibly requires to be reminded that you have got three toes yourself...one on one foot, two on the other."

"Ha! ha! ha!" shouted the queen triumphantly.

The councillor, encouraged by this mark of favour, went on.

"It seems to me, Your Royal Highness, it would greatly endear you to your future people, proving to them that you are not the lesser one of themselves that you had the misfortune to be born of a sun-mother, if you were to command upon yourself the comparatively slight operation which, in a more extended form, you so wisely meditate with regard to your future princess."

"Ha! ha! ha!" laughed the queen louder than before, and the king and the minister joined in the laugh. Noears growled, and for a few moments the others continued to express their enjoyment of his discomfiture.

The queen was the only one Jonny could see with any distinctness. She sat sideway to him, and the light of the fire shone full upon her face. He could not consider her handsome. Her nose was certainly broader at the end than its extreme length, and her eyes, instead of being horizontal, were set up like two perpendicular eggs, one on the broad, the other on the small end. Her mouth was no bigger than a small buttonhole until she laughed, when it stretched from ear to ear...only to better show, her ears were torn and too near her cheeks.

Anxious to hear everything they might say, Jonny ventured to slide down a smooth part of the rock just under him, to a projection below, upon which he thought to rest. But whether he was not careful enough, or the projection gave way, down he came with a rush on the floor of the cavern, bringing with him a great rumbling shower of stones.

The lowlifes jumped from their seats in more anger than consternation, for they had never yet seen anything to be afraid of in their palace. But when they saw Jonny with his PG&E pickaxe in his hand their rage was mingled with fear, for they took him for the first of an invasion of topsiders. The king notwithstanding drew himself up to his full height of five feet, spread himself to his full breadth of three and a half, for he was the handsomest and squarest of all the lowlifes, and strutting up to Jonny, planted himself with outspread feet before him, and said with dignity:

"Pray what right have you in my palace?"

"The right of necessity, Your Majesty," answered Jonny. "I got lost and didn't know where I was wandering to."

"How did you get in?"

"By a hole in the street."

"But you are a PG&E worker! Look at your pickaxe!"

Jonny did look at it, answering:

"I came upon it lying on the ground a little way from here. I tumbled over some wild beasts who were playing with it. Look, Your Majesty." And Jonny showed him how he was scratched and bitten.

The king was pleased to find him behave more politely than he had expected from what his people had told him concerning young topsiders, for he attributed it to the power of his own presence; but he did not therefore feel friendly to the intruder.

"You will oblige me by walking out of my dominions at once," he said, well knowing what a mockery lay in the words.

"Sure, if Your Majesty will give me a guide," said Jonny.

"I will give you a thousand," said the king with a scoffing air of magnificent liberality.

"One will be quite sufficient," said Jonny.

But the king uttered a strange shout, half halloo, half roar, and in rushed lowlifes till the cave was swarming. He said something to the first of them which Jonny could not hear, and it was passed from one to another till in a moment the farthest in the crowd had evidently heard and understood it. They began to gather about him in a way he did not relish, and he retreated towards the wall. They pressed upon him.

"Stand back," said Jonny, grasping the pickaxe tighter by his knee.

They only grinned and pressed closer. Jonny bethought himself and began to rap.

"Ten, twenty, thirty...
You're all so dirty!
Twenty, thirty, forty...
And the odds ain't very sporty!
Thirty, forty, fifty...
You're all so bad and snifty!
Forty, fifty, sixty...
Beast and man all so mixty!
Fifty, sixty, seventy...

The lowlifes fell back a little when he began, and made horrible grimaces all through the rhyme, as if eating something so disagreeable that it set their teeth on edge and gave them the creeps; but whether it was that the rhyming words were most of them no words at all, for, a new rhyme being considered the more efficacious, Jonny had made it on the spur of the moment, or whether it was that the presence of the king and queen gave them courage, I cannot tell; but the moment the rap was over they crowded on him again, and out shot a hundred long arms, with a multitude of thick nailless fingers at the ends of them, to lay hold upon him. Then Jonny heaved up the axe. But being as gentle as courageous and not wishing to kill any of them, he turned the end which was square and blunt like a hammer, and with that came down a great blow on the head of the lowlife nearest him. Hard as the heads of all lowlifes are, he thought he must feel that. And so he did, no doubt; but he only gave a horrible cry, and sprung at Jonny's throat. Jonny, however, drew back in time, and just at that critical moment remembered the vulnerable part of the lowlife body. He made a sudden rush at the king and stamped with all his might on His Majesty's feet. The king gave a most unkingly howl and almost fell into the fire. Jonny then rushed into the crowd, stamping right and left. The lowlifes drew back, howling on every side as he approached, but they were so crowded that few of those he attacked could escape his tread; and the shrieking and roaring that filled the cave would have appalled Jonny but for the good hope it gave him. They were tumbling over each other in heaps in their eagerness to rush from the cave, when a new assailant suddenly faced him... the queen, with flaming eyes and expanded nostrils, her hair standing half up from her head, rushed at him. She trusted in her shoes: they were huge...like Army boots. Jonny would have endured much rather than hurt a woman, even if she was a lowlife; but here was an affair of life and death: forgetting her shoes, he made a great stamp on one of her feet. But she instantly returned it with very different effect, causing him frightful pain, and almost disabling him. His only chance with her would have been to attack the Army boots with the pickaxe, but before he could think of that she had caught him up in her arms and was rushing with him across the cave. She dashed him into a hole in the wall, with a force that almost stunned him. But although he could not move, he was not too far gone to hear her great cry, and the rush of multitudes of soft feet, followed by the sounds of something heaved up against the rock; after which came a multitudinous patter of stones falling near him. The last had not ceased when he grew very faint, for his head had been badly cut, and at last insensible.

When he came to himself there was perfect silence about him, and utter darkness, but for the merest glimmer in one tiny spot. He crawled to it, and found that they had heaved a slab against the mouth of the hole, past the edge of which a poor little gleam found its way from the fire. He could not move it a hairbreadth, for they had piled a great heap of stones and bricks against it. He crawled back to where he had been lying, in the faint hope of finding the pickaxe. But after a vain search he was at last compelled to acknowledge himself in an evil plight. He sat down and tried to think, but soon fell fast asleep.

Chapter 19

He must have slept a long time, for when he awoke he felt wonderfully restored...indeed almost well...and very hungry. There were voices in the outer cave.

Once more, then, it was night; for the lowlifes slept during the day and went about their affairs during the night.

In the universal and constant darkness of their dwelling they had no reason to prefer the one arrangement to the other; but from aversion to the sun-people topsiders they chose to be busy when there was less chance of their being met either by the works below, when they were burrowing, or by the people of the city above, when they were feeding their faces. And indeed it was only when the sun was away that the outside of the city was sufficiently like their own dismal regions to be endurable to their mole eyes, so thoroughly had many of them become unaccustomed to any light beyond that of their own fires and torches.

Jonny listened, and soon found that they were talking of him.

"How long will it take?" asked Noears.

"Not many days, I should think," answered the king. "They are poor feeble creatures, those topsiders, and want to be always eating. We can go a week at a time without food, and be all the better for it; but I've been told they eat two or three times every day! Can you believe it? They must be quite hollow inside...not at all like us, nine-tenths of whose bulk is solid flesh and bone. Yes...I judge a week of starvation will do for him."

"If I may be allowed a word," interposed the queen, "...and I think I ought to have some voice in the matter..."

"The wretch is entirely at your disposal, my spouse," interrupted the king. "He is your property. You caught him yourself. We should never have done it."

The queen laughed. She seemed in far better humour than the night before.

"I was about to say," she resumed, "that it does seem a pity to waste so much fresh meat."

"What are you thinking of, my love?" said the king. "The very notion of starving him implies that we are not going to give him any meat, either salt or fresh."

"I'm not such a stupid as that comes to," returned Her Majesty. "What I mean is that by the time he is starved there will hardly be a picking upon his bones."

The king gave a great laugh.

"Well, my spouse, you may have him when you like," he said. "I don't fancy him for my part. I am pretty sure he is tough eating."

"That would be to honour instead of punish his insolence," returned the queen. "But why should our poor creatures be deprived of so much nourishment? Our little dogs and cats and pigs and small reptiles would enjoy him very much."

"You are the best of housekeepers, my lovely queen!" said her husband. "Let it be so by all means. Let us have our people in, and get him out and kill him at once. He deserves it. The mischief he might have brought upon us, now that he had penetrated so far as our most retired citadel, is incalculable. Or rather let us tie him hand and foot, and have the pleasure of seeing him torn to pieces by full torchlight in the Great Hall."

"Better and better!" cried the queen and the prince together, both of them clapping their hands. And the prince made an ugly noise with his heavy lips, just as if he had intended to be one at the feast.

"But," added the queen, bethinking herself, "he is so

troublesome. For poor creatures as they are, there is something about those topsiders that is very troublesome. I cannot imagine how it is that with such superior strength and skill and understanding as ours, we permit them to exist at all. Why do we not destroy them entirely, and use their buildings at our pleasure? Of course we don't want to live in their horrid sunlight! It is far too glaring for our quieter and more refined tastes. But we might use much of their world as a sort of outhouse, you know. Even our creatures' eyes might get used to it, and if they did grow blind that would be of no consequence, provided they grew fat as well. But we might even keep their great cows and other creatures, and then we should have a few more luxuries, such as fresh cream and cheese, which as present we only taste occasionally, when our brave men have succeeded in carrying some off from their supermarkets or farms."

"It is worth thinking of," said the king; "and I don't know why you should be the first to suggest it, except that you have a positive genius for conquest. But still, as you say, there is something very troublesome about them; and it would be better, as I understand you to suggest, that we should starve him for a day or two first, so that he may be a little less frisky when we take him out."

"Once there was a lowlife
Living in a hole;
Busy did he keep his wife
Who he said had no soul."

"What's that horrible noise?" cried the queen shuddering from pot-metal head to Army boots.

"I declare," said the king with solemn indignation, "it's the topsider in the hole!"

"Stop that disgusting noise!" cried the crown prince valiantly, getting up and standing in front of the heap of stones and bricks, with his face toward Jonny's prison. "Do now, or I'll break your head."

"Go for it," shouted Jonny, and began singing again:

"Once there was a lowlife,

Living in a hole..."

"I really cannot bear it," said the queen. "If I could only get at his horrid toes with my slippers again!"

"I think we had better go to bed!" said the king.

"It's not time to go to bed," said the queen.

"I would if I was you," said Jonny.

"Impertinent wretch!" said the queen, with the utmost scorn in her voice.

"An impossible 'if'," said His Majesty with dignity.

"Quite," returned Jonny, and began singing again:

"Go to bed,

Lowlife, do,

Help the queen

Take off her shoe.

If you do,

It will disclose

A horrid set

Of sprouting toes."

"What a lie!" roared the queen in a rage.

"By the way, that reminds me," said the king, "that for as long as we have been married, I have never seen your feet, Queen. I think you might take off your shoes when you go to bed! They positively hurt me sometimes."

"I will do as I like," retorted the queen sulkily.

"You ought to do as your own hubby wishes you," said the king.

"I will not," said the queen.

"Then I insist upon it," said the king.

Apparently His Majesty approached the queen for the purpose of following the advice given by Jonny, for the latter heard a scuffle, and then a great roar from the king.

"Will you be quiet, then?" said the queen wickedly.

"Yes, yes, Queen. I only meant to coax you."

"Hands off!" cried the queen triumphantly. "I'm going to bed. You may come when you like. But as long as I am queen I will sleep in my shoes. It is my royal privilege. Noears, go to bed."

"I'm going," said Noears sleepily.

"So am I," said the king.

"Come along, then," said the queen; "and mind you are good, or I'll..."

"Oh, no, no, no!" screamed the king in the most supplicating of tones.

Jonny heard only a muttered reply in the distance; and then the cave was quite still.

They had left the fire burning, and the light came through brighter than before. Jonny thought it was time to try again if anything could be done. But he found he could not get even a finger through the chink between the slab and the rock. He gave a great rush with his shoulder against the slab, but it yielded no more than if it had been part of the rock. All he could was to sit down and think again.

By and by he came to the resolution to pretend to be dying, in the hope they might take him out before his strength was too much exhausted to let him have a chance. Then, for the creatures, if he could but find the pickaxe again, he would have no fear of them; and if it were not for the queen's horrid shoes, he would have no fear at all.

Meantime, until they should come again at night, there was nothing for him to do but forge new raps, now his only weapons. He had no intention of using them at present, of course; but it was well to have a stock, for he might live to want them, and the manufacture of them would help to while away the time.

Chapter 20

That same morning early, the little rich girl woke in a terrible fright. There was a hideous noise in her room...of creatures snarling and hissing and racketing about as if they were fighting. The moment she came to herself, she remembered something she had never thought of again...what her grandmother told her to do when she was frightened. She immediately took off her ring and put it under her pillow. As she did so she fancied she felt a finger and thumb take it gently from under her palm. "It must be my grandmother!" she said to herself, and the thought gave her such courage that she stopped to put on her dainty little slippers before running from the room. While doing this she caught sight of a long cloak of sky-blue, thrown over the back of a chair by the bedside. She had never seen it before, but it was evidently waiting for her. She put it on, and then, feeling with the forefinger of her right hand, soon found her grandmother's thread, which she proceeded at once to follow, expecting it would lead her straight up the old stair. When she reached the door she found it went down and ran along the floor, so that she had almost to crawl in order to keep a hold of it. Then, to her surprise, and somewhat to her dismay, she found that instead of leading her toward the stair it turned in quite the opposite direction. It led her through certain narrow passages towards the kitchen, turning aside ere she reached it, and guiding her to a door which communicated with a small back yard. Some of the maids were already up, and this door was standing open. Across the yard the thread still ran along the ground, until it brought her to a door in the wall which opened upon the street. When she had passed through, the thread rose to about half her height, and she could hold it with ease as she walked. It led her straight up the hill.

The cause of her alarm was less frightful than she supposed. The cook's great black cat, pursued by the housekeeper's terrier, had bounced against her bedroom door, which had not been properly fastened, and the two had burst into the room together and commenced a battle royal. How the nurse came to sleep through it was a mystery, but I suspect the old lady had something to do with it.

It was a clear warm morning. The wind blew deliciously over the hills from the Pacific. Here and there she saw a late primrose in a windowbox but she did not stop to call upon them. The sky was mottled with small clouds. The sun was not yet up, but some of their fluffy edges had caught his light, and hung out orange and gold-coloured fringes upon the air. The dew lay in round drops upon parked cars, and hung like tiny diamond earrings from the sidewalk covers of the shops along her path.

"How lovely that bit of gossamer is!" thought the little rich girl, looking at a long undulating line that shone at some distance from her up the hill. It was not the time for gossamers though; and Tiffany soon discovered that it was her own thread she saw shining on before her in the light of the morning. It was leading her she knew not whither; but she had never in her life been out before sunrise, and everything was so fresh and cool and lively and full of something coming, that she felt too happy to be afraid of anything.

After leading her up a good distance, the thread turned to the left, and down the road upon which she and Nursie had met Jonny. But she never thought of that, for now in the morning light, with its far outlook over the city, no road could have been more open and airy and cheerful. She could see the street almost to the horizon, along which she had so often watched her father and his car come shining, with the horn-blast cleaving the air before them; and it was like a companion to her. Down and down the road went, then up, and then down and then up again, getting steep and more rugged as it went; and still along the street went the silvery thread, and still along the thread went Tiffany's little rosy-tipped forefinger. By and by she came to a little stream in a gutter that jabbered and prattled down the hill, and up the side of the stream went both sidewalk and thread. And still the road grew rougher and rougher, and the city grew wilder, till Tiffany began to think she was going a very long way from home; and when she turned to look back she saw that the level city had vanished and the rough brick city had closed in about her. But still on went the thread, and on went the little rich girl. Everything around her was getting brighter and brighter as the sun came nearer; till at length his first rays all at once alighted on the top of a car before her, like some golden creature fresh from the sky. Then she saw that the little stream in the gutter ran out of a hole in the street beside that car, that the sidewalk did not go past the wall that the hole came out of, and that the thread was leading her straight up to it. A shudder ran through her from head to foot when she found that the thread was actually taking her into the hole out of which the stream of water ran. It ran out babbling joyously, but she had to go in.

She did not hesitate. Right into the hole she went, which was high enough to let her walk without stooping. For a little way there was a brown glimmer, but at the first turn it all but ceased, and before she had gone many paces she was in total darkness. Then she began to be frightened indeed. Every moment she kept feeling the thread backwards and forwards, and as she went farther and farther into the darkness of the great hollow city, she kept thinking more and more about her grandmother, and all that she had said to her, and how kind she had been, and how beautiful she was, and all about her lovely room, and the fire of roses, and the great lamp that sent its light through stone walls. And she became more and more sure that the thread could not have gone there of itself, and that her grandmother must have sent it. But it tried her dreadfully when the path went down very steep, and especially when she came to places where she had to go down rough stairs, and even sometimes a ladder. Through one narrow passage after another, over jumps of rock and sand and clay, the thread guided her, until she came to a small hole through which she had to creep. Finding no change on the other side, "Shall I ever get back?" she thought, over and over again, wondering at herself that she was not ten times more frightened, and often feeling as if she were only walking in the story of a dream. Sometimes she heard the noise of water, a dull gurgling inside the rock. By and by she heard the sounds of blows, which came nearer and nearer; but again they grew duller, and almost died away. In a hundred directions she turned, obedient to the guiding thread.

At last she spied a dull red shine, and came up to the mica window, and thence away and round about, and right into a cavern, where glowed the red embers of a fire. Here the thread began to rise. It rose as high as her head and higher still. What should she do if she lost her hold? She was pulling it down! She might break it! She could see it far up, glowing as red as her fire opal in the light of the embers.

But presently she came to a huge heap of stones, piled in a slope against the wall of the cavern. On these she climbed, and soon recovered the level of the thread...only to find however, that the next moment, it vanished through the heap of stones, and left her standing on it, with her face to the solid rock. For one terrible moment she felt as if her grandmother had forsaken her. The thread which the television had spun, which her grandmother had sat in the moonlight and spun again for her, which she had tempered in the rose fire and tied to her opal ring, had left her...had gone where she could no longer follow it...had brought her into a horrible cavern, and there left her! She was forsaken indeed!

"When shall I wake?" she said to herself in an agony, but the same moment knew that it was no dream. She threw herself upon the heap, and began to cry. It was well she did not know what creatures, one of them with Army boots on her feet, were lying in the next cave. But neither did she know who was on the other side of the slab.

At length the thought struck her that at least she could follow the thread backwards, and thus get out of the underground, and home. She rose at once, and found the thread. But the instant she tried to feel it backwards, it vanished from her touch. Forwards, it led her hand up to the heap of stones...backwards it seemed nowhere. Neither could she see it as before in the light of the fire. She burst into a wailing cry, and again threw herself down on the stones and bricks.

Chapter 21

A s the little rich girl lay and sobbed she kept feeling the thread mechanically, following it with her finger many times up to the stones in which it disappeared. By and by she began, still mechanically, to poke her finger in after it between the stones as far as she could. All at once it came to her head that she might remove some of the stones and see where the thread went next. Almost laughing at herself for never having thought of this before, she jumped to her feet. Her fear vanished; once more she was certain her grandmother's thread could not have brought her there just to leave her there; and she began to throw away the stones from the top as fast as she could, sometimes two or three at a handful, sometimes taking both hands to lift one. After clearing them away a little, she found that the thread turned and went straight downwards. Hence, as the heap sloped a good deal, growing of course wider towards the base, she had to throw away a multitude of stones and bricks to follow the thread. But this was not all, for she soon found that the thread, after going straight down for a little way, turned first sideways in one direction, then sideways in another, and then shot, at various angles, hither and thither inside the heap, so that she began to be afraid that to clear the thread she must remove the whole huge gathering. She was dismayed at the very idea, but, losing no time, set to work with a will; and with aching back, and bleeding fingers and hands, she worked on, sustained by the pleasure of seeing the heap slowly diminish and begin to show itself on the opposite side of the fire.

Another thing which helped to keep up her courage was that, as often as she uncovered a turn of the thread, instead of lying loose upon the stones, it tightened up; this made her sure that her grandmother was at the end of it somewhere.

She had got about halfway down when she started, and nearly fell with fright.   Close to her ears as it seemed, a voice broke out singing:

"Jabber, bother, smash!

You'll look like a crash.

Jabber, smash, bother!

Then will come my father.

Smash, bother, jabber..."

Here Jonny stopped, either because he could not find a rap to "jabber", or because he remembered what he had forgotten when he woke up at the sound of Tiffany's labours, that his plan was to make the lowlifes think he was getting weak.   But he had uttered enough to let Tiffany know who he was.

"It's Jonny!" she cried joyfully.

"Hush! Hush!" came Jonny's voice again from somewhere. "Speak softly."

"Why? You were singing loud!" said Tiffany.

"Yes. But they know I am here, and they don't know you are. Who are you?"

"I'm Tiffany," answered the little rich girl. "I know who you are quite well. You're Jonny."

"Why, how did you get in here, Tiffany?"

"My great-great-grandmother sent me; and I think I've found out why. You can't get out, I suppose?"

"No, I can't. What are you doing?"

"Clearing away a huge heap of stones."

"There's a rich lady!" exclaimed Jonny, in a tone of delight, still speaking in little more than a whisper. "I can't think how you got here, though."

"My grandmother sent me after her thread."

"I don't know what you mean," said Jonny; "but so you're there, it doesn't much matter."

"Oh, yes, it does!" returned Tiffany. "I should never have been here but for her."

"You can tell me all about it when we get out, then. There's no time to lose now," said Jonny.

And Tiffany went to work, as fresh as when she began.

"There's such a lot of stones!" she said. "It will take me a long time to get them all away."

"How far on have you got?" asked Jonny.

"I've got about half away, but the other half is ever so much bigger."

"I don't think you will have to move the lower half. Do you see a slab laid up against the wall?"

Tiffany looked, and felt about with her hands, and soon perceived the outlines of the slab.

"Yes," she answered, "I do."

"Then, I think," rejoined Jonny, "when you have cleared the slab about halfway down, or a little more, I shall be able to push it over."

"I must follow my thread," returned Tiffany, "whatever I do."

"What do you mean?" exclaimed Jonny.

"You will see when you get out," answered the little rich girl, and went on harder than ever.

But she was soon satisfied that what Jonny wanted done and what the thread wanted done were one and the same thing. For she not only saw that by following the turns of the thread she had been clearing the face of the slab, but that, a little more than halfway down, the thread went through the chink between the slab and the wall into the place where Jonny was confined, so that she could not follow it any farther until the slab was out of her way. As soon as she found this, she said in a right joyous whisper:

"Now, Jonny! I think if you were to give a great push, the slab would tumble over."

"Stand quite clear of it, then," said Jonny, "and let me know when you are ready."

Tiffany got off the heap, and stood on one side of it.

"Now, Jonny!" she cried.

Jonny gave a great rush with his shoulder against it. Out tumbled the slab on the heap, and out crept Jonny over the top of it.

"You've saved my life, Tiffany!" he whispered.

"Oh, Jonny! I'm so glad! Let's get out of this horrid place as fast as we can."

"That's easier said than done," returned the young man.

"Oh, no! It's quite easy," said Tiffany. "We have only to follow my thread. I am sure that it's going to take us out now."

She had already begun to follow it over the fallen slab into the hole, while Jonny was searching the floor of the cavern for the PG&E pickaxe.

"Here it is!" he cried. "No, it's not!" he added, in a disappointed tone. "What can it be, then? I declare it's a torch. Great! It's better almost than my pickaxe. Much better if it weren't for those Army boots!" he went on, as he lighted the torch by blowing the last embers of the expiring fire.

When he looked up, with the lighted torch casting a glare into the great darkness of the huge cavern, he caught sight of Tiffany disappearing in the hole out of which he had himself just come.

"Where are you going there?" he cried. "That's not the way out. That's where I couldn't get out."

"I know that," whispered Tiffany. "But this is the way my thread goes, and I must follow it."

"What nonsense the child talks!" said Jonny to himself. "I must follow her, though, and see that she comes to no harm. She will soon find she can't get out that way, and then she will come with me."

So he crept over the slab once more into the hole with his torch in his hand. But when he looked about in it, he could see her nowhere. And now he discovered that although the hole was narrow, it was much longer than he had supposed; for in one direction the roof came down very low, and the hole went off in a narrow passage, of which he could not see the end. The little rich girl must have crept in there. He got on his knees and one hand, holding the torch with the other, and crept after her. The hole twisted about, in some parts so low that he could hardly get through, in others so high that he could not see the roof, but everywhere it was narrow...far too narrow for a lowlife adult to get through, and so I presume they never thought that Jonny might. He was beginning to feel very uncomfortable lest something should have befallen the little rich girl, when he heard her voice almost close to his ear, whispering:

"Aren't you coming, Jonny?"

And when he turned the next corner there she stood waiting for him.

"I knew you couldn't go wrong in that narrow hole, but now you must keep by me, for here is a great wide place," she said.

"I can't understand it," said Jonny, half to himself, half to Tiffany.

"Never mind," she returned. "Wait till we get out."

Jonny, utterly astonished that she had already got so far, and by a path he had known nothing of, thought it better to let her do as she pleased.

"Holy smokes," he said again to himself, "I don't know nothing about the way out; and she seems to think she does know something about it, though how she should is beyond me. So she's just as likely to find her way as I am, and as she insists on taking the lead, I must follow. We can't be much worse off than we are, anyhow."

Reasoning thus, he followed her a few steps, and came out in another great cavern, across which Tiffany walked in a straight line, as confidently as if she knew every step of the way. Jonny went on after her, flashing his torch about, and trying to see something of what lay around them. Suddenly he started back a pace as the light fell upon something close by which Tiffany was passing. It was a platform of rock raised a few feet from the floor and covered with sheepskins, upon which lay two horrible figures asleep, at once recognized by Jonny as the king and queen of the lowlifes. He lowered his torch instantly lest the light should awake them. As he did so it flashed upon his pickaxe, lying by the side of the queen, whose hand lay close by the handle of it

"Stop one moment," he whispered. "Hold my torch, and don't let the light on their faces."

Tiffany shuddered when she saw the frightful creatures, whom she had passed without observing them, but she did as he requested, and turning her back, held the torch low in front of her. Jonny drew his pickaxe carefully away, and as he did so spied one of her feet, projecting from under the skins. The great clumsy Army boot, exposed thus to his hand, was a temptation not to be resisted. He laid hold of it, and, with cautious efforts, drew it off. The moment he succeeded, he saw to his astonishment that what he had sung in ignorance, to annoy the queen, was actually true: she had six horrible toes. Overjoyed at his success, and seeing by the huge bump in the sheepskins where the other foot was, he proceeded to lift them gently, for, if he could only succeed in carrying away the other boot as well, he would be no more afraid of the lowlifes than of so many flies. But as he pulled at the second boot the queen gave a growl and sat up in bed. The same instant the king awoke also and sat up beside her.

"Run, Tiffany!" cried Jonny, for though he was not now in the least afraid for himself, he was for the little rich girl.

Tiffany looked once round, saw the fearful creatures awake, and like the wise little rich girl she was, dashed the torch on the ground and extinguished it, crying out:

"Here, Jonny, take my hand."

He darted to her side, forgetting neither the queen's boot nor his pickaxe, and caught hold of her hand, as she sped fearlessly where her thread guided her. They heard the queen give a great bellow; but they had a good start, for it would be some time before they could get torches lighted to pursue them. Just as they thought they saw a gleam behind them, the thread brought them to a very narrow opening, through which Tiffany crept easily, and Jonny with difficulty.

"Now," said Jonny, "I think we shall be safe."

"Of course we shall," returned Tiffany.

"Why do you think so?" asked Jonny.

"Because my grandmother is taking care of us."

"That's all nonsense," said Jonny. "I don't know what you mean."

"Then if you don't know what I mean what right have you to call it nonsense?" asked the little rich girl, a little offended.

"Excuse me, Tiffany," said Jonny; "I didn't mean to upset you."

"Of course not," returned the little rich girl. "But why do you think we shall be safe?"

"Because the king and queen are far too stout to get through that hole."

"There might be ways round," said the little rich girl.

"You got that right: we are not out of it yet," acknowledged Jonny.

"But what do you mean by the king and queen?" asked the little rich girl. "I should never call such creatures as those a king and a queen."

"Their own people do, though," answered Jonny.

The little rich girl asked more questions, and Jonny, as they walked leisurely along, gave her a full account, not only of the character and habits of the lowlifes, so far as he knew them, but of his own adventures with them, beginning from the very night after that in which he had met her and Nursie upon the mountain. When he had finished, he begged Tiffany to tell him how it was that she had come to his rescue. So Tiffany too had to tell a long story, which she did in rather a roundabout manner, interrupted by many questions concerning things she had not explained. But her tale, as he did not believe more than half of it, left everything as unaccountable to him as before, and he was nearly as much perplexed as to what he must think of the little rich girl. He could not believe that she was deliberately telling stories, and the only conclusion he could come to was that Nursie had been playing the child tricks, inventing no end of lies to frighten her for her own purposes.

"But how ever did Nursie come to let you go into the city alone?" he asked.

"Nursie knows nothing about it. I left her fast asleep...at least I think so. I hope my grandmother won't let her get into trouble, for it wasn't her fault at all, as my grandmother very well knows."

"But how did you find your way to me?" persisted Jonny.

"I told you already," answered Tiffany; "by keeping my finger upon my grandmother's thread, as I am doing now."

"You don't mean you've got the thread there?"

"Of course I do. I have told you so ten times already. I have hardly...except when I was removing the stones...taken my finger off it. There!" she added, guiding Jonny's hand to the thread. "You feel it yourself...don't you?"

"I feel nothing at all," replied Jonny.

"Then what can be the matter with your finger? I feel it perfectly. To be sure it is very thin, and in the sunlight looks just like the thread of a spider, though there are many of them twisted together to make it...but for all that I can't think why you shouldn't feel it as well as I do."

Jonny was too polite to say he did not believe there was any thread there at all. What he did say was:

"Well, I don't know..."

"I do, though, and you must be glad of that, for it will do for both of us."

"We're not out yet," said Jonny.

"We soon shall be," returned Tiffany confidently. And now the thread went downwards, and led Tiffany's hand to a hole in the floor of the cavern, whence came a sound of running water which they had been hearing for some time.

"It goes into the ground now, Jonny," she said, stopping.

He had been listening to another sound, which his practiced ear had caught long ago, and which also had been growing louder. It was the noise the lowlife miners made at their work, and they seemed to be at no great distance now. Tiffany heard it the moment she stopped.

"What is that noise?" she asked. "Do you know, Jonny?"

"Yes. It is the lowlifes digging and burrowing," he answered.

"And you don't know what they do it for?"

"No; I haven't the least idea. Would you like to see them?" he asked, wishing to have another try after their secret.

"If my thread took me there, I shouldn't much mind; but I don't want to see them, and I can't leave my thread. It leads me down into the hole, and we had better go at once."

"Very well. Do you want me to go first?" said Jonny.

"No; better not. You can't feel the thread," she answered, stepping down through a narrow break in the floor of the cavern. "Oh!" she cried, "I am in the water. It is running strong...but it is not deep, and there is just room to walk. Make haste, Jonny."

He tried, but the hole was too small for him to get in.

"Go on a little bit," he said, shouldering his pickaxe.

In a few moments he had cleared a larger opening and followed her. They went on, down and down with the running water, Jonny getting more and more afraid it was leading them to some terrible gulf in the heart of the earth under the city. In one or two places he had to break away the rock to make room before even Tiffany could get through...at least without hurting herself. But at length they spied a glimmer of light, and in a minute more they were almost blinded by the full sunlight, into which they emerged. It was some little time before the little rich girl could see well enough to discover that they stood in her own garden, close by the seat on which she and her father had sat that afternoon. They had come out by the channel of the little steam in the rock. She danced and clapped her hands with delight.

"Now, Jonny!" she cried, "won't you believe what I told you about my grandmother and her thread?"

For she had felt all the time that Jonny was not believing what she told him.

"There!...don't you see it shining on before us?" she added.

"I don't see anything," persisted Jonny.

"Then you must believe without seeing," said the little rich girl; "for you can't deny it has brought us out of the darkness."

"I can't deny we are out of the darkness, and I should be very ungrateful indeed to deny that you had brought me out of it."

"I couldn't have done it but for the thread," persisted Tiffany.

"That's the part I don't understand."

"Well, come along, and Nursie will get you something to eat. I am sure you must want it very much."

"Indeed I do. But my father and mother will be so anxious about me, I must hurry...first up the hill to tell my mother, and then down into the garage again to let my father know."

"Very well, Jonny; but you can't get out without coming this way, and I will take you through the house, for that is nearest."

They met no one by the way, for, indeed, as before, the people were here and there and everywhere searching for the little rich girl. When they got in Tiffany found that the thread, as she had half expected, went up the old staircase, and a new thought struck her. She turned to Jonny and said:

"My grandmother wants me. Do come up with me and see her. Then you will know that I have been telling you the truth. Do come...to please me, Jonny. I can't bear you should think what I say is not true."

"I never doubted you believed what you said," returned Jonny. "I only thought you had some fancy in your head that was not correct."

"But do come, dear Jonny."

The little black carwasher could not withstand this appeal, and though he felt shy in what seemed to him a huge grand house, he yielded, and followed her up the stair.

Chapter 22

U p the stair then they went, and the next and the next, and through the long rows of empty rooms, and up the little top stair, Tiffany growing happier and happier as she ascended. There was no answer when she knocked at length at the door of the workroom, nor could she hear any sound of the television, and once more her heart sank within her, but only for one moment, as she turned and knocked at the other door.

"Come in," answered the sweet voice of her grandmother, and Tiffany opened the door and entered, followed by Jonny.

"You darling!" cried the lady, who was seated by a fire of red roses mingled with white. "I've been waiting for you, and indeed getting a little anxious about you, and beginning to think whether I had not better go and fetch you myself."

As she spoke she took the little rich girl in her arms and placed her upon her lap. She was dressed in white now, and looking if possible more lovely than ever.

"I've brought Jonny, Grandmother. He wouldn't believe what I told him and so I've brought him."

"Yes...I see him. He is a good boy, Jonny, and a brave boy. Aren't you glad you've got him out?"

"Yes, Grandmother. But it wasn't very good of him not to believe me when I was telling him the truth."

"People must believe what they can, and those who believe more must not be hard upon those who believe less. I doubt if you would have believed it all yourself if you hadn't seen some of it."

"Ah! Yes, Grandmother, I dare say. I'm sure you are right. But he'll believe now."

"I don't know that," replied the grandmother.

"Won't you, Jonny?" said Tiffany, looking round at him as she asked the question.

He was standing in the middle of the floor, staring, and looking strangely bewildered. This she thought came of his astonishment at the beauty of the lady.

"Make a bow to my grandmother, Jonny," she said.

"I don't see any grandmother," answered Jonny rather gruffly.

"Don't see my grandmother, when I'm sitting in her lap?" exclaimed the little rich girl.

"No, I don't," reiterated Jonny, in an offended tone.

"Don't you see the lovely fire of roses...white ones amongst them this time?" asked Tiffany, almost as bewildered as he.

"No, I don't" answered Jonny, almost sulkily.

"Nor the blue bed? Nor the rose-coloured counterpane? Nor the beautiful light, like the moon, hanging from the roof?"

"You're making fun of me, Tiffany; and after what we have come through together this day, I don't think it is kind of you," said Jonny, feeling very much hurt.

"Then what do you see?" asked Tiffany, who perceived at once that for her not to believe him was at least as bad as for him not to believe her.

"I see a big, bare, garret-room...like the one in mother's apartment, only big enough to take the whole apartment itself in, and leave a good margin all round," answered Jonny.

"And what more do you see?"

"I see a tub, and a heap of musty straw, and a withered apple, and a ray of sunlight coming through a hole in the middle of the roof and shining on your head, and making all the place look a curious dusky brown. I think you had better drop it, Tiffany, and go down to the nursery, like a good girl."

"But don't you hear my grandmother talking to me?" asked Tiffany, almost crying.

"No. I hear the cooing of a lot of pigeons. If you won't come down, I will go without you. I think that will be better anyhow, for I'm sure nobody who met us would believe a word we said to them. They would think we made it all up. I don't expect anybody but my own father and mother to believe me. They know I wouldn't tell a story."

"And yet you won't believe me, Jonny?" expostulated the little rich girl, now fairly crying with vexation and sorrow at the gulf between her and Jonny.

"No. I can't, and I can't help it," said Jonny, turning to leave the room.

"What shall I do, Grandmother?" sobbed the little rich girl, turning her face round upon the lady's bosom, and shaking with suppressed sobs.

"You must give him time," said her grandmother; "and you must be content not to be believed for a while. It is very hard to bear; but I have had to bear it, and shall have to bear it many a time yet. I will take care of what Jonny thinks of you in the end. You must let him go now."

"You're not coming, are you?" asked Jonny.

"No, Jonny; my grandmother says I must let you go. Turn to the right when you get to the bottom of all the stairs, and that will take you to the hall where the great door is."

"Oh! I don't doubt I can find my way...without you, Tiffany, or your old granny's thread either," said Jonny quite rudely.

"Oh! Jonny! Jonny!"

"I wish I had gone home at once. I'm very much obliged to you, Tiffany, for getting me out of that hole, but I wish you hadn't made a fool of me afterwards."

He said this as he opened the door, which he left open, and, without another word, went down the stair. Tiffany listened with dismay to his departing footsteps. Then turning again to the lady:

"What does it all mean, Grandmother?" she sobbed, and burst into fresh tears.

"It means, my love, that I did not mean to show myself. Jonny is not yet able to believe some things. Seeing is not believing...it is only seeing. You remember I told you that if Nursie were to see me, she would rub her eyes, forget the half she saw, and call the other half nonsense."

"Yes; but I should have thought Jonny..."

"You are right. Jonny is much farther on than Nursie, and you will see what will come of it. But in the meantime you must be content, I say, to be misunderstood for a while. We are all very anxious to be understood, and it is very hard not to be. But there is one thing much more necessary."

"What is that, Grandmother?"

"To understand other people."

"Yes, Grandmother. I must be fair...for if I'm not fair to other people, I'm not worth being understood myself. I see. So as Jonny can't help it, I will not be upset with him, but just wait."

"There's my own dear child," said her grandmother, and pressed her close to her bosom.

"Why weren't you in your workroom when we came up, Grandmother?" asked Tiffany, after a few moments' silence.

"If I had been there, Jonny would have seen me well enough. But why should I be there rather than in this beautiful room?"

"I thought you would be watching television."

"I've nobody to watch for just at present. I never watch without knowing for whom I am watching."

"That reminds me...there is one thing that puzzles me," said the little rich girl: "how are you to get the thread out of the darkness under the city again? Surely you won't have to make another for me? That would be such a trouble!"

The lady set her down and rose and went to the fire. Putting in her hand, she drew it out again and held up the shining ball between her finger and thumb.

"I've got it now, you see," she said, coming back to the little rich girl, "all ready for you when you want it."

Going to her cabinet, she laid it in the same drawer as before.

"And here is your ring," she added, taking it from the little finger of her left hand and putting it on the forefinger of Tiffany's right hand.

"Oh, thank you, Grandmother! I feel so safe now!"

"You are very tired my child," the lady went on. "Your hands are hurt with the stones, and I have counted nine bruises on you. Just look what you are like."

And she held up to her a little mirror which she had brought from the cabinet. The little rich girl burst into a merry laugh at the sight. She was so draggled with the stream, and dirty with creeping through narrow places, that if she had seen the reflection without knowing it was a reflection, she would have taken herself for some slum child whose face was washed and hair combed about once in a month. The lady laughed too, and lifting her again upon her knee, took off her cloak and nightgown. Then she carried her to the side of the room. Tiffany wondered what she was going to do with her, but asked no questions...only starting a little when she found that she was going to lay her in the large silver bath; for as she looked into it, again she saw no bottom, but the stars shining miles away, as it seemed, in a great blue gulf. Her hands closed involuntarily on the beautiful arms that held her, and that was all.

The lady pressed her once more to her bosom, saying:

"Do not be afraid, my child."

"No, Grandmother," answered the little rich girl, with a little gasp; and the next instant she sank in the clear cool water.

When she opened her eyes, she saw nothing but a strange lovely blue over and beneath and all about her. The lady and the beautiful room had vanished from her sight, and she seemed utterly alone. But instead of being afraid, she felt more than happy...perfectly blissful. And from somewhere came the voice of the lady, singing a strange sweet song, of which she could distinguish every word; but of the sense she had only a feeling...no understanding. Nor could she remember a single line after it was gone. It vanished, like the poetry in a dream, as fast as it came. In after years, however, she would sometimes fancy that snatches of melody suddenly rising in her brain must be little phrases and fragments of the air of that song; and the very fancy would make her happier, and abler to do her duty.

How long she lay in the water she did not know. It seemed a long time...not from weariness but from pleasure. But at last she felt the beautiful hands lay hold of her, and through the gurgling water she was lifted out into the lovely room. The lady carried her to the fire, and sat down with her in her lap, and dried her tenderly with the softest towel. It was so different from Nursie's drying. When the lady had done, she stooped to the fire, and drew from it her nightgown, as white as snow.

"How delicious!" exclaimed the little rich girl. "It smells of all the roses in the world, I think."

When she stood up on the floor she felt as if she had been made over again. Every bruise and all weariness were gone, and her hands were soft and whole as ever.

"Now I am going to put you to bed for a good sleep," said her grandmother.

"But what will Nursie be thinking? And what am I to say to her when she asks me where I have been?"

"Don't trouble yourself about it. You will find it all come right," said her grandmother, and laid her into the blue bed, under the rosy counterpane.

"There is just one thing more," said Tiffany. "I am a little anxious about Jonny. As I brought him into the house, I ought to have seen him safe on his way home."

"I took care of all that," answered the lady. "I told you to let him go, and therefore I was bound to look after him. Nobody saw him, and he is now eating a good dinner in his mother's apartment far up in the city."

"Then I will go to sleep," said Tiffany, and in a few minutes she was fast asleep.

Chapter 23

Jonny went up the hill neither whistling nor singing for he was vexed with Tiffany for taking him in, as he called it; and he was vexed with himself for having spoken to her so angrily. His mother gave a cry of joy when she saw him, and at once set about getting him something to eat, asking him questions all the time, which he did not answer so cheerfully as usual. When his meal was ready, she left him to eat it, and hurried to phone the garage to let his father know he was safe. When she came back, she found him fast asleep upon her bed; nor did he wake until his father came home in the evening.

"Now, Jonny," his mother said as they sat at supper, "tell us the whole story from beginning to end, just as it all happened."

Jonny obeyed, and told everything to the point where they came out upon the lawn in the garden of the rich man's house.

"And what happened after that?" asked his mother. "You haven't told us all. You ought to be very happy at having got away from those demons, and instead of that I never saw you so gloomy. There must be something more. Besides, you do not speak of that lovely child as I should like to hear you. She saved your life at the risk of her own, and yet somehow you don't seem to think much of it."

"She talked such nonsense!" answered Jonny, "and told me a pack of things that weren't a bit true; and I can't get over it."

"What were they?" asked his father. "Your mother may be able to throw some light upon them."

Then Jonny made a clean breast of it, and told them everything.

They all sat silent for some time, pondering the strange tale. At last Jonny's mother spoke.

"You confess, my boy," she said, "there is something about the whole affair you do not understand?"

"Yes, of course, Mother," he answered. "I cannot understand how a child knowing nothing about the city, or even that I was shut up in the lowlife cave, should come all that way alone, straight to where I was; and then, after getting me out of the hole, lead me out of the darkness too, where I should not have known a step of the way if it had been as light as in the open air."

"Then you have no right to say what she told you was not true. She did take you out, and she must have had something to guide her: why not a thread as well as a rope, or anything else? There is something you cannot explain, and her explanation may be the right one."

"It's not an explanation at all, Mother; and I can't believe it."

"That may be only because you do not understand it. If you did, you would probably find it was an explanation, and believe it thoroughly. I don't blame you for not being able to believe it, but I do blame you for fancying such a child would try to deceive you. Why should she? Depend upon it, she told you all she knew. Until you had found a better way of accounting for it all, you might at least have been more sparing of your judgement."

"That is what something inside me has been saying all the time," said Jonny, hanging down his head. "But what do you make of the grandmother? That is what I can't get over. To take me up to an old garret, and try to persuade me against the sight of my own eyes that it was a beautiful room, with blue walls and silver stars, and no end of things in it, when there was nothing there but an old tub and a withered apple and a heap of straw and a sunbeam! It was too bad! She might have had some old woman there at least to pass for her precious grandmother!"

"Didn't she speak as if she saw those other things herself, Jonny?"

"Yes. That's what bothers me. You would have thought she really meant and believed that she saw every one of the things she talked about. And not one of them there! It was too bad."

"Perhaps some people can see things other people can't see, Jonny," said his mother very gravely. "I think I will tell you something I saw myself once...only perhaps you won't believe me either!"

"Oh, Mother!" cried Jonny, bursting into tears; "I don't deserve that, surely!"

"But what I am going to tell you is very strange," persisted his mother; "and if having heard it you were to say I must have been dreaming, I don't know that I should have any right to be vexed with you, though I know at least that I was not asleep."

"Do tell me, Mother. Perhaps it will help me to think better of the little rich girl."

"That's why I am tempted to tell you," replied his mother. "But first, I may as well mention that, according to old whispers, there is something more than common about the rich man's family; and the queen was of the same blood, for they were cousins of some degree. There were strange stories told concerning them...all good stories...but strange, very strange. What they were I cannot tell, for I only remember the faces of my grandmother and my mother as they talked together about them. There was wonder and awe...not fear...in their eyes, and they whispered, and never spoke aloud. But what I saw myself was this: Your father was going to work in the garage one night, and I had been down with his supper. It was soon after we were married, and not very long before you were born. He came with me to the mouth of the garage, and left me to go home alone, for I knew the way almost as well as the floor of our own apartment. It was pretty dark, and some parts of the road where the buildings blocked out the moon and the streetlights had burned out were nearly quite dark. But I got along perfectly well enough, Jonny, to where the road is crossed by the freeway overpass. When I got there, I was suddenly surrounded by about half a dozen of the lowlifes, the first I had ever seen, although I had heard tell of them often enough. One of them blocked the sidewalk, and they all began tormenting and teasing me in a way it makes me shudder to think of even now."

"If I had only been with you!" cried father and son in a breath.

The mother gave a funny little smile, and went on.

"They had some of their horrible creatures with them too, and I must confess I was dreadfully frightened. They had torn my clothes very much when suddenly a great white soft light shone upon me. I looked up. A broad ray, like a shining road, came down from a large globe of silvery light, not very high up, indeed not quite so high as the nearby buildings...so it could not have been a new star or another moon or a UFO or anything of that sort. The lowlifes dropped persecuting me, and looked dazed, and I thought they were going to run away, but presently they began again. The same moment, however, down the sidewalk from the globe of light came a bird, shining like silver in the sun. It gave a few rapid flaps first, and then, with its wings straight out, shot sliding down the slope of the light. It looked to me just like a white pigeon. But whatever it was, when the lowlifes caught sight of it coming straight down upon them, they took to their heels and scampered away across the city, leaving me safe, only much frightened. As soon as it had sent them off, the bird went gliding again up the light, and the moment it reached the globe the light disappeared, just as if a shutter had been closed over a window, and I saw it no more. But I had no more trouble with the lowlifes that night or ever after."

"How strange!" exclaimed Jonny.

"Yes, it was strange; but I can't help believing it, whether you do or not," said his mother.

"It's exactly as your mother told it to me the very next morning," said the father.

"You don't think I'm doubting my own mother?" cried Jonny.

"There are other people in the world quite as well worth believing as your own mother," said his mother. "I don't know that she's so much the fitter to be believed that she happens to be your mother, Mr. Jonny. There are mothers far more likely to tell lies than the little girl I saw talking to the primroses a few weeks ago. If she were to lie I should begin to doubt my own word."

"But little rich girls have told lies as well as other people," said Jonny.

"Yes, but not little rich girls like that child. She's a good girl, I am certain, and that's more than being a little lady. Depend upon it you will have to be sorry for behaving so to her, Jonny. You ought at least to have held your tongue."

"I am sorry now," answered Jonny.

"You ought to go and tell her so, then."

"I don't see how I could manage that. They wouldn't let a black kid like me have a word with her alone; and I couldn't tell her before that nurse of hers She'd be asking a ton of questions, and I don't know how many the little rich girl would like me to answer. She told me that Nursie didn't know anything about her coming to get me out of the underworld. I am certain she would have prevented her somehow if she had known it. But I may have a chance before long, and meantime I must try to do something for her. I think, Father, I have got on the track at last."

"Have you, indeed, my boy?" said Earl Mo. "I am sure you deserve some success; you have worked very hard for it. What have you found out?"

"It's difficult, you know, Father, inside the underworld, especially in the dark, and not knowing what turns you have taken, to tell the lay of things outside."

"Impossible, my boy, without a chart, or at least a compass," returned his father.

"Well, I think I have nearly discovered in what direction the lowlifes are mining. If I am right, I know something else that I can put to it, and then one and one will make three."

"They very often do, Jonny, as we ought to be very well aware. Now tell us, son, what the two things are, and see whether we can guess at the same third as you."

"I don't see what that has to do with the little rich girl," interposed his mother.

"I will soon let you see that, Mother. Perhaps you may think me foolish, but until I am sure there is nothing in my present fancy, I am more determined than ever to go on with my observations. Just as we came to the channel by which we got out, I heard the miners at work somewhere near...I think down below us. Now since I began to watch them, they have mined a good half-mile, in a straight line; and so far as I am aware, they are working in no other part of the city. But I never could tell in what direction they were going. When we came out in the rich man's garden, however, I thought at once whether it was possible they were working towards the rich man's house; and what I want to do tonight is to make sure whether they are or not. I will take a light with me..."

"Oh, Jonny," cried his mother, "then they will see you."

"I'm no more afraid of them now than I was before," rejoined Jonny, "now that I've got this precious boot. They can't make another such in a hurry, and one bare foot will do for my purpose. Woman as she may be, I won't spare her next time. But I shall be careful with my light, for I don't want them to see me. I won't stick it out past my feet."

"Go on, then, and tell us what you mean to do."

"I mean to take a bit of paper with me and a pencil, and go in at the mouth of the gutter by which we came out. I shall mark on the paper as near as I can the angle of every turning I take until I find the lowlifes at work, and so get a good idea in what direction they are going. If it should prove to be nearly parallel with the drain, I shall know it is towards the rich man's house they are working."

"And what if you should? How much wiser will you be then?"

"Wait a minute, Mother dear. I told you that when I came upon the royal family in the cave, they were talking of their prince...Noears, they called him...marrying a topsider woman...that means one of us...one with toes to her feet. Now in the speech one of them made that night at their great gathering, of which I heard only a part, he said that peace would be secured for a generation at least by the pledge the prince would hold for the good behaviour of 'her' relatives: that's what he said, and he must have meant the topsider woman the prince was to marry. I am quite sure the king is much too proud to wish his son to marry any but a rich girl, and much too knowing to fancy that his having a poor woman for a wife would be of any great advantage to them."

"I see what you are driving at now," said his mother.

"But," said his father, "the rich people of this city would order the Army in and blow up every tunnel and chamber under the earth before they would have any of their young women become the wife of a lowlife, even if he were ten times a prince."

"And I think," said Jonny, "if they once get her, they would tell her rich father they would kill her unless he consented to the marriage."

"They might say so," said his father, "but they wouldn't kill her; they would keep her alive for the sake of the hold it gave them over her father. Whatever he did to them, they would threaten to do the same to the girl."

"And they are bad enough to torment her just for their own amusement...I know that," said his mother.

"Anyhow, I will keep a watch on them, and see what they are up to," said Jonny. It's too horrible to think of. I can't let myself do it. But they won't have her...at least if I can help it. So, Mother dear...my clue is all right...will you get me a bit of paper and a pencil and some food, and I will set out at once. I saw a place where I can climb over the wall of the garden quite easily."

"You must mind and keep out of the way of the men on watch," said his mother.

"That I will. I don't want them to know anything about it. They would spoil it all. The lowlifes would only try some other plan...they are such obstinate creatures! I shall take good care, Mother. They won't kill and eat me either, if they should come upon me. So you needn't mind them."

His mother got him what he had asked for, and Jonny set out. Close beside the door by which the little rich girl left the garden for the city stood a great buttress, and by climbing it Jonny got over the wall. He tied his clue to a stone just inside the channel of the stream drain, and took his PG&E pickaxe with him. He had not gone far before he encountered a horrid creature coming towards the mouth. The spot was too narrow for two of almost any size or shape, and beside Jonny had no wish to let the creature pass. Not being able to use his pickaxe, however, he had a severe struggle with him, and it was only after receiving many bites, some of them bad, that he succeeded in killing the creature with his pocketknife. Having dragged him out, Jonny made haste to get in again before another should stop up the way.

I need not follow him farther in this night's adventure. He returned to his breakfast, satisfied that the lowlifes were mining in the direction of the rich man's house...on so low a level that their intention must, he thought, be to burrow under the walls of the house, and rise up inside it...in order, he fully believed, to lay hands on the little rich girl, and carry her off for a wife to their horrid Noears.

Chapter 24

When the little rich girl awoke from the sweetest of sleeps, she found her nurse bending over her, the housekeeper looking over the nurse's shoulder, and the laundry-maid looking over the housekeeper's. The room was full of women-servants; and the bodyguards, with a long column of servants behind them, were peeping, or trying to peep in at the door of the nursery.

"Are those horrid creatures gone?" asked the little rich girl, remembering first what had terrified her in the morning.

"You naughty, naughty little girl!" cried Nursie.

Her face was very pale, with red streaks in it, and she looked as if she were going to shake her; but Tiffany said nothing...only waited to hear what should come next.

"How could you get under the clothes like that, and make us all think you were lost! And keep it up all day too! You are the most obstinate child! It's anything but fun to us, I can tell you!"

It was the only way the nurse could account for her disappearance.

"I didn't do that, Nursie," said Tiffany, very quietly.

"Don't tell stories!" cried her nurse quite rudely.

"I shall tell you nothing at all," said Tiffany.

"That's just as bad," said the nurse.

"Just as bad to say nothing at all as to tell stories?" exclaimed the little rich girl. "I will ask my father about that. He won't say so. And I don't think he will like you to say so."

"Tell me directly what you mean by it!" screamed the nurse, half-wild with anger at the little rich girl, and fright at the possible consequences to herself.

"When I tell you the truth, Nursie," said the little rich girl, who somehow did not feel at all angry, "you say to me 'Don't tell stories': it seems I must tell stories before you will believe me."

"You are very rude, young lady," said the nurse.

"You are so rude, Nursie, that I will not speak to you again till you are sorry. Why should I, when I know you will not believe me?" returned the little rich girl.

For she did know perfectly well that if she were to tell Nursie what she had been about, the more she went on to tell her, the less would she believe her.

"You are the most provoking child!" cried her nurse. "You deserve to be well punished for your wicked behaviour."

"Please, Mrs. Housekeeper," said the little rich girl, "will you take me to your room, and keep me till my father comes? I will ask him to come as soon as he can.

Everyone stared at these words. Up to this moment they had all regarded her as little more than a baby.

But the housekeeper was afraid of the nurse, and sought to patch matters up, saying:

"I am sure, my dear, that Nursie did not mean to be rude to you."

"I do not think my father would wish me to have a nurse who spoke to me as Nursie does. If she thinks I tell lies, she had better either say so to my father, or go away. Mr. Marshall, will you take charge of me?"

"With the greatest of pleasure, young lady," answered the leader of the bodyguards, walking with his great stride into the room. The crowd of servants made eager way for him, and he bowed low before the little rich girl's bed. "I shall call at once to tell your father that you desire his presence. When you have chosen one of these under-servants to wait upon you, I shall order the room to be cleared."

"Thank you very much, Mr. Marshall," said the little rich girl, and her eye glanced towards a rosy-cheeked girl who had lately come to the house as a scullery-maid.

But when Nursie saw the eyes of her dear little rich girl going in search of another instead of her, she fell upon her knees by the bedside, and burst into a great cry of distress.

"I think, Mr. Marshall," said the little rich girl, "I will keep Nursie. But I put myself under your care; and you need not trouble my father until I speak to you again. Will you all please to go away? I am quite safe and well, and I did not hide myself for the sake either of amusing myself, or of troubling my home's staff. Nursie, will you please dress me."

Chapter 25

Everything was for some time quiet above ground. The rich man was still away in a distant part of his business empire. The bodyguards kept watching about the house. They had been considerably astonished by finding at the foot of the rock in the garden the hideous body of the lowlife creature killed by Jonny; but they came to the conclusion that it had been slain in the sewers and had crept out there to die. The body was turned over to the police, who lost it and never reported it to the press for fear of panic. Except for an occasional glimpse of a live one they saw nothing to cause alarm about. Jonny kept watching underground, and the lowlifes kept burrowing deeper into the earth. As long as they went deeper there was, Jonny judged, no immediate danger.

To Tiffany the summer was as full of pleasure as ever, and for a long time, although she often thought of her grandmother during the day, and often dreamed about her at night, she did not see her. The toys and the flowers were as much her delight as ever, and she made as much friendship with the local children she met on the streets as Nursie would permit; but Nursie had very foolish notions concerning the dignity of a little rich girl, not understanding that the truest young lady is just the one who loves all her brothers and sisters best, and who is most able to do them good by being humble towards them. At the same time she was considerably altered for the better in her behaviour to the little rich girl. She could not help seeing that she was no longer a mere child, but wiser than her age would account for. She kept foolishly whispering to the servants, however...sometimes that the little rich girl was not right in her mind, sometimes that she was too good to live, and other nonsense of the same sort.

All this time Jonny had to be sorry, without a chance of confessing, that he had behaved so unkindly to the little rich girl. This perhaps made him the more diligent in his endeavours to serve her. His mother and he often talked on the subject, and she comforted him, and told him she was sure he would some day have the opportunity he so much desired.

Here I should like to remark, for the girl and little rich girls in general, that it is a low and contemptible thing to refuse to confess a fault, or even an error. If a true young lady has done wrong, she is always uneasy until she has had an opportunity of throwing the wrongness away from her by saying: "I did it; and I wish I had not; and I am sorry for having done it." So you see there is some ground for supposing that Jonny was not a carwasher only, but in many ways a very rich young man as well. A prince in his own right. Many such instances have been known in the world's history.

At length, however, he began to see signs of a change in the proceedings of the lowlife excavators: they were going no deeper, but had commenced running on a level; and he watched them, therefore, more closely than ever. All at once, one night, coming to a slope of very hard rock, they began to ascend along the inclined plane of its surface. Having reached its top, they went again on a level for a night or two, after which they began to ascend once more, and kept on at a pretty steep angle. At length Jonny judged it time to transfer his observation to another quarter, and the next night he did not go underground from the garage at all; but leaving his PG&E pickaxe and clue at home, and taking only his usual lumps of bread and butter, went down the hill to the rich man's house. He climbed over the wall, and remained in the garden the whole night, creeping on hands and knees from one spot to the other, and lying at full length with his ear to the ground, listening. But he heard nothing except the tread of the bodyguards as they marched about, whose observation, as the night was cloudy and there was no moon, he had little difficulty in avoiding. For several following nights he continued to haunt the garden and listen, but with no success.

At length, early one evening, whether it was that he had got careless of his own safety, or that the growing moon had become strong enough to expose him, his watching came to a sudden end. He was creeping from behind the rock where the stream ran out, for he had been listening all round it in the hope it might convey to his ear some indication of the whereabouts of the lowlife miners, when just as he came into the moonlight on the lawn, a whiz in his ear and a blow upon his leg startled him. He instantly squatted in the hope of eluding further notice. But when he heard the sound of running feet, he jumped up to take the chance of escape by flight. He fell, however, with a keen shoot of pain, for a bullet had wounded his leg, and the blood was now streaming from it. He was instantly laid hold of by two or three of the bodyguards. It was useless to struggle, and he submitted in silence.

"It's a boy!" cried several of them together, in a tone of amazement. "I thought it was one of those lowlife creatures."

"What are you doing here?"

"Going to have a rough night, apparently," said Jonny, laughing, as the men shook him.

"Impertinence will do you no good. You have no business here in the rich man's grounds, and if you don't tell us the truth of what you are up to, you will be charged as a thief."

"Why, what else could he be?" said one.

"He might have been out playing around, you know," suggested one of the black bodyguards.

"I see no good in trying to excuse him. He has no business here, anyhow."

"Let me go then, please," said Jonny.

"But we don't please...not unless you tell us what you were really doing here."

"I don't feel quite sure whether I can trust you," said Jonny.

"We are the rich man's own bodyguards," said the leader courteously, for he was taken with Jonny's appearance and courage.

"Well, I will tell you all about it...if you will promise to listen to me and not do anything crazy."

"I call that cool!" said one of the party, laughing. "He will tell us what mischief he was up to, if we promise to do as he wants."

"I wasn't up to any mischief," said Jonny.

But ere he could say more he turned faint, and fell senseless on the grass. Then first they discovered that the bullet they had shot, taking him for one of the lowlife creatures, had wounded him.

They carried him into the house and laid him down in the hall. The report spread that they had caught a robber, and the servants crowded in to see the villain. Amongst the rest came the nurse. The moment she saw him she exclaimed with indignation:

"I declare it's the same young rascal of a carwasher that was rude to me and the little rich girl in the city. He actually wanted to kiss Tiffany. I took good care of that...the wretch! And he was prowling about...was he? Just like his impudence!"

The little rich girl being fast asleep, she could misrepresent at her pleasure.

When he heard this, the leader of the bodyguards, although he had considerable doubt of its truth, resolved to keep Jonny a prisoner until they could turn him over to the police to search into the affair. So, after they had brought him round a little, and attended to his wound, which was rather a bad one, they laid him, still exhausted from the loss of blood, upon a mattress in a disused room...one of those already so often mentioned...and locked the door, and left him. This did not last long, however. Soon the police came and took Jonny to the prison ward of a nearby hospital. There he passed a troubled night, and in the morning the doctors found him talking wildly. In the evening he came to himself, but felt very weak, and his leg was exceedingly painful. Wondering where he was, and seeing one of the policemen in the room, he began to question him, and soon recalled the events of the preceding night.

Tiffany and the Lowlifes

As he was himself unable to watch any more, he told the policeman all he knew about the lowlifes, and begged him to tell the rich man's bodyguards, and stir them up to watch with tenfold vigilance; but whether it was that he did not talk quite coherently, or that the whole thing appeared incredible, certainly the man concluded that Jonny was only raving still, and tried to coax him into holding his tongue. This, of course, annoyed Jonny dreadfully, who now felt in his turn what it was not to be believed, and the consequence was that his fever returned, and by the time when, at his persistent entreaties, somebody in charge was called, there could be no doubt that he was raving. They did for him what they could, and promised everything he wanted, but with no intention of fulfillment. At last he went to sleep, and when at length his sleep grew profound and peaceful, they left him, locked the door of the room, and withdrew, intending to revisit him early in the morning.

Chapter 26

That same night several of the servants were having a chat together before going to bed. "What can that noise be?" said one of the housemaids, who had been listening for a moment or two.

"I've heard it the last two nights," said the cook. "If there were any about the place, I should have taken it for rats, but my cat keeps them far enough."

"I've heard, though," said the scullery-maid, "that rats move about in great companies sometimes. There may be an army of them invading us. I've heard the noises yesterday and today too."

"It'll be grand fun, then, for my Mr. Cat and Mrs. Housekeeper's Rin-Tin-Can," said the cook. "They'll be friends for once in their lives, and fight on the same side. I'll engage Mr. Cat and Rin-Tin-Can; together they will put to flight any number of rats."

"It seems to me," said the nurse, "that the noises are much too loud for that. I have heard them all day, and my little rich girl has asked me several times what they could be. Sometimes they sound like distant thunder, and sometimes like the noises you hear in the BART from those horrid underground workers."

"I shouldn't wonder," said the cook, "if it was PG&E workers after all. They may have come on some hole under the city through which the noises reach to us. They are always boring and blasting and breaking, you know."

As he spoke, there came a great rolling rumble beneath them, and the house quivered. They all started up in affright, and rushing to the hall found the bodyguards in consternation also. They had sent to wake their leader, who said from their description that it must have been an earthquake, an occurrence which was not that rare in that country; and then went to bed again, strange to say, and fell fast asleep without once thinking of Jonny, or associating the noises they had heard with what he had told them. He had not believed Jonny. If he had, he would at once have thought of what he had said, and would have taken precautions. As they heard nothing more, they concluded that Mister Marshall was right, and that the danger was over for perhaps another few years. The fact, as discovered afterwards, was that the lowlifes had, in working up a second sloping face of stone, arrived at a huge block which lay under the cellars of the house, within the line of the foundations. It was so round that when they succeeded, after hard work, in dislodging it without blasting, it rolled thundering down the slope with a bounding, jarring roll, which shook the foundations of the house. The lowlifes were themselves dismayed at the noise, for they knew, by careful spying and measuring, that they must now be very near, if not under the rich man's house, and they feared giving an alarm. They, therefore, remained quiet for a while, and when they began to work again, they no doubt thought themselves very fortunate in coming upon a vein of sand which filled a winding fissure in the rock on which the house was built. By scooping this away they came out in the rich man's wine cellar.

No sooner did they find where they were, than they scurried back again, like rats into their holes, and running at full speed to the lowlife palace, announced their success to the king and queen with shouts of triumph. In a moment the lowlife royal family and the whole lowlife people were on their way in hot haste to the rich man's house, each eager to have a share in the glory of carrying off that same night the little rich girl Tiffany.

The queen went stumping along in one Army boot and one bare foot. This could not have been pleasant, and readers may wonder that, with such skillful workmen about her, she had not yet replaced the boot carried off by Jonny. As the king, however, had more than one ground of objection to her Army boots, he no doubt took advantage of the discovery of her toes, and threatened to expose her deformity if she had another made. I presume he insisted on her being content with skin socks, and allowed her to wear the remaining Army boot on the present occasion only because she was going out to war.

They soon arrived in the rich man's wine cellar, and regardless of its huge vessels, of which they did not know the use, proceeded at once, but as quietly as they could, to force the door that led upwards.

Chapter 27

When Jonny fell asleep he began at once to dream. He thought he was ascending the streets of the hill from the mouth of the garage, whistling and rapping when he came upon a woman and child who had lost their way; and from that point he went on dreaming everything that had happened to him since he thus met the little rich girl and Nursie; how he had watched the lowlifes, how he had been taken by them, how he had been rescued by the little rich girl; everything, indeed, until he was wounded, captured, and imprisoned by the police. And now he thought he was lying wide awake where they had laid him, when suddenly he heard a great thundering sound.

"The lowlifes are coming!" he said. "They didn't believe a word I told them! The lowlifes'll be carrying off the little rich girl from under their stupid noses! But they won't!"

He jumped up, as he thought, and began to dress, but, to his dismay, found that he was still lying in bed.

"Now then, I will!" he said. "Here goes! I am up now!"

But yet again he found himself snug in bed. Twenty times he tried, and twenty times he failed; for in fact he was not awake, only dreaming that he was. At length in an agony of despair, fancying he heard the lowlifes all around him, he gave a great cry. Then there came, as he thought, a hand upon the lock of the hospital door. It opened, and, looking up, he saw a lady with white hair, carrying a silver box in her hand, enter the room. She came to his bed, he thought, stroked his head and face with cool, soft hands, took the dressing from his leg, rubbed it with something that smelt like roses, and then waved her hands over him three times. At the last wave of her hands everything vanished, he felt himself sinking into the profoundest slumber, and remembered nothing more until he awoke in earnest.

The setting moon was throwing a feeble light through the window of the hospital room...but somehow Jonny knew that things were not right in the rich man's house. He sprang from his bed, hurried on some of his clothes, not forgetting his shoes, which were armed with nails. He went to the door and found it unlocked. Opening it slowly, he saw the policeman left to guard outside was fast asleep. So Jonny crept past the man and out of the hospital. From there he ran all the way back to the rich man's house.

As Jonny entered the open gate in the front, there was soft heavy multitudinous stamping, a clashing and clanging of weapons, the voices of men and the cries of women, mixed with a hideous bellowing, which sounded victorious. The lowlifes were in the house! As he turned from the driveway onto the steps he found one of the bodyguards who had been knocked out. Spying the man's long knife and his gun, Jonny picked them up and rushed up the stairs, guided by the sounds of strife, which grew louder and louder.

When he entered the front door he found the whole place swarming. All the lowlifes of the city seemed gathered there. He rushed amongst them, shouting:

"One, two,

I'm as bad as you!

Three, four,

Your mama's a whore!"

And with every rhyme he came down a great stamp upon a foot, cutting at the same time their faces...executing, indeed, a sword dance of the wildest description. Away scattered the lowlifes in every direction...into closets, up stairs, into chimneys, up on rafters, and down to the cellars. Jonny went on stamping and slashing and shooting and singing, but saw nothing of the people of the house until he came to the Great Hall, in which, the moment he entered it, arose a great lowlife shout. The last of the bodyguards, the leader himself, was on the floor buried beneath a wallowing crowd of lowlifes. For, while each bodyguard was busy defending himself as well as he could, by shots and stabs in the thick bodies of the lowlifes, for each had soon found their heads all but invulnerable, the queen had attacked the leader's legs and feet with her horrible Army boot, and he was soon down; but the leader had got his back to the wall and stood out longer. The lowlifes would have torn them all to pieces, but the king had given orders to carry them away alive, and over each of them, in twelve groups, was standing a knot of lowlifes, while as many as could find room were sitting upon their prostrate bodies.

Jonny burst in dancing and gyrating and stamping and singing like a small incarnate whirlwind.

"They came from a hole, sir,
From one of a million holes:
Why should their shoes have soles, sir,
When they've got no souls?
But she upon her foot, sir,
Has an Army boot shoe:
The strongest military boot, sir,
That bullet won't pass through."

The queen gave a howl of rage and dismay; and before she recovered her presence of mind, Jonny, having begun with the group nearest him, had eleven of the bodyguards on their legs again.

"Stamp on their feet!" he cried as each man rose, and in a few minutes the hall was nearly empty, the lowlifes running from it as fast as they could, howling and shrieking and limping, and cowering every now and then as they ran to cuddle their wounded feet in their hard hands, or to protect them from the frightful stamp-stamp of the armed men.

And now Jonny approached the group which, in trusting in the queen and her boot, kept their guard over the prostrate leader. The king sat on the leader's head, but the queen stood in front, like an infuriated cat, with her perpendicular eye gleaming green, and her hair standing half up from her horrid head. Her heart was quaking, however, and she kept moving about her skin-socked foot with nervous apprehension. When Jonny was within a few paces, she rushed at him, made one tremendous stamp at his opposing foot, which happily he withdrew in time, and caught him round the waist, to dash him on the marble floor. But just as she caught him, he came down with all the weight of his steel-shod shoe upon her skin-socked foot, and with a hideous howl she dropped him, squatted on the floor, and took her foot in both her hands. Meanwhile the rest rushed on the king and the bodyguard, sent them flying, and lifted the prostrate leader, who was all but pressed to death. It was some moments before he recovered breath and consciousness.

"Where's Tiffany?" cried Jonny, again and again.

No one knew, and off they all rushed in search of her. Through every room in the house they went, but nowhere was she to be found. Neither was one of the servants to be seen. But Jonny, who had kept to the lower part of the house, which was now quiet enough, began to hear a confused sound as of a distant hubbub, and set out to find where it came from. The noise grew as his sharp ears guided him to a stair and so to the wine cellar. It was full of lowlifes, whom the butler was supplying with wine as fast as he could pour it.

While the queen and her party had encountered the bodyguards, Noears with another company had gone off to search the house. They captured everyone they met, and when they could find no more, they hurried away to carry them safe to the caverns below. But when the butler, who was amongst them, found that their path lay through the wine cellar, he bethought himself of persuading them to taste the wine, and, as he had hoped, they no sooner tasted than they wanted more. The routed lowlifes, on their way below, joined them, and when Jonny entered they were all, with outstretched hands, in which were vessels of every description from saucepan to silver cup, pressing around the butler, who sat at the tap of a huge cask, filling and filling. Jonny cast one glance around the place before commencing his attack, and saw in the farthest corner a terrified group of the domestics unwatched, but cowering without courage to attempt their escape. Amongst them was the terror-stricken face of Nursie; but nowhere could he see the little rich girl. Seized with the horrible conviction that Noears had already carried her off, he rushed amongst them, unable for wrath to sing any more, but stamping and cutting with greater fury than ever.

"Stamp on their feet; stamp on their feet!" he shouted, and in a moment the lowlifes were disappearing through the hole in the floor like rats and mice.

They could not vanish so fast, however, but that many more lowlifes' feet had to go limping back over the underground ways of the city that morning.

Presently, however, they were reinforced from above by the king and his party, with the redoubtable queen at their head. Finding Jonny again busy amongst her unfortunate subjects, she rushed at him once more with the rage of despair, and this time gave him a bad bruise on the foot. Then a regular stamping fight got up between them, Jonny, with the point of the knife, keeping her from clasping her mighty arms about him, as he watched his opportunity of getting once more a good stamp at her skin-socked foot. But the queen was more wary as well as more agile than hitherto.

The rest meantime, finding their adversary thus matched for the moment, paused in their headlong hurry, and turned to the shivering group of women in the corner. As if determined to emulate his father and have a sun-woman of some sort to share his future throne, Noears rushed at them, caught up Nursie, and sped with her to the hole. She gave a great shriek, and Jonny heard her, and saw the plight she was in. Gathering all his strength, he gave the queen a sudden cut across the face with his weapon, came down, as she started back, with all his weight on the proper foot, and sprung to Nursie's rescue. The prince had two defenseless feet, and on both of them Jonny stamped just as he reached the hole. He dropped his burden and rolled shrieking into the earth. Jonny made one stab at him as he disappeared, caught hold of the senseless Nursie, and having dragged her back to the corner, there mounted guard over her, preparing once more to encounter the queen. Her face streaming with blood, and her eyes flashing green lightning through it, she came on with her mouth open and her teeth grinning like a tiger's, followed by the king and her bodyguards of the thickest lowlifes. But the same moment in rushed the leader of the rich man's bodyguards and his men, and ran at them stamping furiously. They dared not encounter such an onset. Away they scurried, the queen foremost. Of course, the right thing would have been to take the king and queen prisoners, and hold them hostages for the little rich girl, but they were so anxious to find her that no one thought of detaining them until it was too late.

Having thus rescued the servants, they set about searching the house once more. None of them could give the least information concerning the little rich girl. Nursie was almost silly with terror, and, although scarcely able to walk, would not leave Jonny's side for a single moment. Again he allowed the others to search the rest of the house...where, except a dismayed lowlife lurking here and there, they found no one...while he requested Nursie to take him to the little rich girl's room. She was as submissive and obedient as if he had been the rich man.

He found the bedclothes tossed about, and most of them on the floor, while the little rich girl's garments were scattered all over the room, which was in the greatest confusion. It was only too evident that the lowlifes had been there, and Jonny had no longer any doubt that she had been carried off at the very first of the inroad. With a pang of despair he saw how wrong they had been in not securing the king and queen and prince; but he determined to find and rescue the little rich girl as she had found and rescued him, or meet the worst fate to which the lowlifes could doom him.

Chapter 28

Just as the consolation of this resolve dawned upon his mind and he was turning away for the cellar to follow the lowlifes into their hole, something touched his hand. It was the slightest touch, and when he looked he could see nothing. Feeling and peering about in the grey of the dawn, his fingers came upon a tight thread. He looked again, and narrowly, but still could see nothing. It flashed upon him that this must be the little rich girl's thread. Without saying a word, for he knew no one would believe him any more than he had believed the little rich girl, he followed the thread with his finger, contrived to give Nursie the slip, and was soon out of the house and on the city streets...surprised that, if the thread were indeed the grandmother's messenger, it should have led the little rich girl, as he supposed it must, into the city, where she would be certain to meet the lowlifes rushing back enraged from their defeat. But he hurried on in the hope of overtaking her first. When he arrived, however, at the place where the path turned off for the garage, he found that the thread did not turn with it, but went straight up the other hill. Could it be that the thread was leading him home to his mother's apartment? Could the little rich girl be there? He bounded up the hill like one of the local kittens, and before the sun was up the thread had brought him indeed to his mother's door. There it vanished from his fingers, and he could not find it, search as he might.

The door was on the latch, and he entered. There sat his mother by the heater, and in her arms lay the little rich girl fast asleep.

"Hush, Jonny!" said his mother. "Do not wake her. I'm so glad you're come! I thought the lowlifes must have got you again!"

With a heart full of delight, Jonny sat down at a corner of the heater, on a stool opposite his mother's chair, and gazed at the little rich girl, who slept as peacefully as if she had been in her own bed. All at once she opened her eyes and fixed them on him.

"Oh, Jonny! You've come!" she said quietly. "I thought you would!"

Jonny rose and stood before her with downcast eyes.

"Tiffany," he said, "I am very sorry I did not believe you."

"Oh, never mind, Jonny!" answered the little rich girl. "You couldn't, you know. You do believe me now, don't you?"

"I can't help it now. I ought to have helped it before."

"Why can't you help it now?"

"Because, just as I was going into the underworld to took for you, I got hold of your thread, and it brought me here."

"Then you've come from my house, have you?"

"Yes, I have."

"I didn't know you were there."

"I've been there several hours, I believe."

"And I never knew it! Then perhaps you can tell me why my grandmother has brought me here? I can't think. Something woke me...I didn't know what, but I was frightened, and I felt for the thread, and there it was! I was more frightened still when it brought me out on to the city streets, for I thought it was going to take me into the underworld again, and I like the outside the best. I supposed you were in trouble again, and I had to get you out. But it brought me here instead; and, oh Jonny! Your mother has been so kind to me...just like my own grandmother!"

Here Jonny's mother gave the little rich girl a hug, and the little rich girl turned and gave her a sweet smile, and held up her mouth to kiss her.

"Then you didn't see the lowlifes?" asked Jonny.

"No; I haven't been into the underworld, I told you, Jonny."

"But the lowlifes have been into your house...all over it...and into your bedroom, making such a row!"

"What did they want there? It was very rude of them."

"They wanted you...to carry you off into the underworld with them, for a wife to their prince Noears."

"Oh, how dreadful!" cried the little rich girl, shuddering.

"But you needn't be afraid, you know. Your grandmother takes care of you."

"Ah! You do believe in my grandmother, then? I'm so glad! She made me think you would some day."

All at once Jonny remembered his dream, and was silent, thinking.

"But how did you come to be in my house, and me not know it?" asked the little rich girl.

Then Jonny had to explain everything...how he had watched for her sake, how he had been wounded and shut up by the police, how he heard the noises and could not rise, and how the beautiful old lady had come to him in the hospital, and all that followed.

"Poor Jonny! To lie there hurt and ill, and me never to know it!" exclaimed the little rich girl, stroking his rough hand. "I would have come and nursed you, if they had told me."

"I didn't see you were lame," said his mother.

"Am I, mother? Oh...yes...I suppose I ought to be. That's strange, I've never thought of it since I got up to go down amongst the lowlifes!"

"Let me see the wound," said his mother.

He pulled up his pants leg...when behold, except a great scar, his leg was perfectly sound!

Jonny and his mother gazed in each other's eyes, full of wonder, but Tiffany called out:

"I thought so, Jonny! I was sure it wasn't a dream. I was sure my grandmother had been to see you. Don't you smell the roses? It was my grandmother healed your leg, and sent you to help me."

"No, dear Tiffany," said Jonny; "I wasn't good enough to be allowed to help you: I didn't believe you. Your grandmother took care of you without me."

"She sent you to help my people, anyhow. I wish my papa would come. I do want so to tell him how good you have been!"

"But," said the mother, "we are forgetting how frightened your people must be. You must take Tiffany home at once Jonny...or at least go and tell them where she is."

"Yes, Mother. Only I'm dreadfully hungry. Do let me have some breakfast first. They ought to have listened to me, and then they wouldn't have been taken by surprise as they were."

"That is true, Jonny; but it is not for you to blame them much, you remember?"

"Yes, Mother, I do. Only I must really have something to eat."

"You shall, my son...as fast as I can get it," said his mother, rising and setting the little rich girl on her chair.

But before his breakfast was ready, Jonny jumped up so suddenly as to startle both his companions.

"Mother, Mother!" he cried, "I was forgetting. You must take Tiffany home yourself. I must go and wake my father."

Without a word of explanation, he rushed to the place where his father was sleeping. Having thoroughly roused him with what he told him, he darted out of the apartment.

Chapter 29

He had all at once remembered the resolution of the lowlifes to carry out their second plan upon the failure of the first. No doubt they were already busy, and the city was therefore in the greatest danger of having all of its underground parts flooded and rendered useless...not to speak of the lives of the thousands of workmen, people parking their cars, or people on the BART trains.

When he reached the mouth of the garage, after rousing all the workers within reach, he found his father and a good many more just entering. They all hurried to the tunnel by which he had found a way into the lowlife country. There the foresight of Earl Mo had already collected a great many blocks of stone, with cement, ready for building up the weak place...well enough known to the lowlifes. Although there was not room for more than two to be actually building at once, they managed, by setting all the rest to work in preparing the cement and passing the stones, to finish in the course of the day a huge buttress filling the whole tunnel, and supported everywhere by steel and cement. Before the hour when they usually dropped work, they were satisfied the garage was secure. And a phone call to their friends at several of the underground PG&E tunnels made sure the same was done at other locations under the city.

They had heard lowlife hammers and pickaxes busy all the time, and at length fancied they heard sounds of water they had never heard before. But that was otherwise accounted for when they left the garage; for they stepped out into a tremendous storm which was raging all over the city. The thunder was bellowing, and the lightning lancing out of the huge black clouds which lay above it and hung down their edges of thick mist over their sides. The lightning was breaking out of the city, too, and flashing up into the clouds. From the state of the gutters, now swollen into raging torrents, it was evident the storm had been storming all day.

The wind was blowing as if it would blow him off the streets, but, anxious about his mother and the little rich girl, Jonny darted up through the thick of the tempest. Even if they had not set out before the storm came on, he did not judge them safe, for in such a storm even their poor old apartment building was in danger. Indeed he soon found that but for a huge warehouse against which it was built, and which protected it both from the blasts and the waters, it must have been swept if it was not blown away; for the two torrents into which this warehouse parted the rush of water behind it united on the street corner again in front of the apartment building...two roaring and dangerous streams that moved cars as if they were toys, which his mother and the little rich girl could not possibly have passed. It was with great difficulty that he forced his way through one of them, and up to the door.

The moment he ran upstairs and fell on the latch, through all the uproar of winds and waters came the joyous cry of the little rich girl:

"There's Jonny! Jonny! Jonny!"

She was sitting wrapped in blankets on the bed, his mother trying for the hundredth time to light the heater which had been browned by the lack of power, cut off when the rain brought the lines down. The wooden floor was one mass of wet rug and mud, and the whole place looked wretched. But the faces of the mother and the little rich girl shone as if their troubles only made them the merrier. Jonny burst out laughing at the sight of them.

"I never had such fun!" said the little rich girl, her eyes twinkling and her pretty teeth shining. "How nice it must be to live in an apartment building in the city!"

"It all depends on what kind of landlord you have," said the mother.

"I know what you mean," said Tiffany. "That's the kind of thing my grandmother says."

By the time Earl Mo returned, the storm was nearly over, but the streams were so fierce and so swollen that it was not only out of the question for the little rich girl to go down the hill, but most dangerous for Earl Mo even or Jonny to make the attempt in the gathering darkness.

"They will be dreadfully frightened about you," said Earl Mo to the little rich girl, "but we cannot help it. All the phone lines are even down. We must wait till the morning."

With Jonny's help, a fire was lighted in the old fireplace, and the mother set about making their supper over it; and after supper they all told the little rich girl stories till she grew sleepy. Then Jonny's mother laid her in Jonny's bed, which was in a tiny little garret-room. As soon as she was in bed, through a little window low down in the roof she caught sight of her grandmother's lamp shining far away beneath, and she gazed at the beautiful silvery globe until she fell asleep.

Chapter 30

The next morning the sun rose so bright that Tiffany said the rain had washed his face and let the light out clean. The torrents were still roaring down the side of the hill, but they were so much smaller as not to be dangerous in the daylight. After an early breakfast, Earl Mo went to his work and Jonny and his mother set out to take the little rich girl home. They had difficulty in getting her dry across the gutter streams, and Jonny had again and again to carry her, but at last they got safe on the broader part of the road, and walked gently down towards the rich man's house. And what should they see as they turned the last corner but the rich man's great car driving through the gate!

"Oh, Jonny!" cried Tiffany, clapping her hands right joyfully. "My papa has come."

The moment Jonny heard that, he caught her up in his arms, and set off at full speed, crying:

"Come on, Mother! The rich man may break his heart before he knows that she is safe."

Tiffany clung round his neck and he ran with her like a deer. When he entered the gate into the court, there sat the rich man in his car, with all the people of the house about the door, weeping and hanging their heads. The rich man was not weeping, but his face was white as a dead man's, and he looked as if the life had gone out of him. The bodyguards he had brought with him sat with horror-stricken faces, but eyes flashing with rage, waiting only for the word of the rich man to do something...they did not know what, and nobody knew what.

The day before, the bodyguards belonging to the house, as soon as they were satisfied the little rich girl had been carried away, rushed after the lowlifes into the hole, but found that they had already so skillfully blockaded the narrowest part, not many feet below the cellar, that without miners and their tools they could do nothing. Not one of them knew where any of the other entrances to the underworld lay, and some of these who had set out to find a few had been overtaken by the storm and had not even yet returned. Poor Mister Marshall was especially filled with shame, and almost hoped the rich man would order him fired, for to think of that sweet little face down amongst the lowlifes was unendurable.

When Jonny ran in at the gate with the little rich girl in his arms, they were all so absorbed in their own misery and awed by the rich man's presence and grief, that no one observed his arrival. He went straight up to the rich man, where he sat in the door of his car.

"Papa! Papa!" the little rich girl cried, stretching out her arms to him. "Here I am!"

The rich man started. The color rushed to his face. He gave an inarticulate cry. Jonny held up the little rich girl, and the rich man bent through the door and took her from the young man's arms. As he clasped her to his chest, the big tears went dropping down his cheeks. And such a shout arose from all the bystanders that the startled children outside the gate pranced and capered, and the buildings of the city echoed back the noises. The little rich girl greeted them all as she nestled in her father's arms, and the rich man did not set her down until she had told them all the story. But she had more to tell about Jonny than about herself, and what she did tell about herself none of them could understand except the rich man and Jonny, who stood by the rich man's knee next to the car door. And still as she told what Jonny had done, Mister Marshall and others added to what she told, even Nursie joining in the praises of his courage and energy.

Jonny held his peace, looking quietly up in the rich man's face. And his mother stood on the outskirts of the crowd listening with delight, for her son's deeds were pleasant in her ears, until the little rich girl caught sight of her.

"And there is his mother, Papa!" she said. "See...there. She is such a nice mother, and has been so kind to me!" They all parted asunder as the rich man made a sign to her to come forward. She obeyed, and he gave her his hand, but could not speak.

"And now, Papa," the little rich girl went on, "I must tell you another thing. One night long ago Jonny drove the lowlifes away and brought Nursie and me safe from the city. And I promised him a kiss when we got home, but Nursie wouldn't let me give it to him. I don't want you to scold Nursie, but I want you to tell her that a lady must do as she promises."

"Indeed she must, my child...except when it is wrong," said the rich man. "There, give Jonny a kiss."

And as he spoke he held her towards Jonny.

The little rich girl reached out, threw her arms round Jonny's neck and kissed him on the mouth, saying:

"There Jonny! There's the kiss I promised you!"

Then they all went into the house, and the cook rushed to the kitchen and the servants to their work. Nursie dressed Tiffany in her shiningest clothes, and the rich man put off his rain coat, and put on a fine English wool jacket...and a messenger was sent for Earl Mo and all the garage workers, and there was a great and a grand feast, which continued long after the little rich girl was put to bed.

Chapter 31

A friend of the rich man was an Opera star, who had come over for the party, and was chanting a ballad which he made as he went along playing on the fine concert piano...about the little rich girl and the lowlifes, and the prowess of Jonny, when all at once he ceased, with his eyes on one of the doors of the hall. Thereupon the eyes of the rich man and his guests turned thitherward also. The next moment, through the open doorway came the little rich girl, Tiffany. She went straight up to her father, with her right hand stretched out a little sideways, and her forefinger, as her father and Jonny understood, feeling its way along the invisible thread. The rich man took her on his knee, and she said in his ear:

"Papa, do you hear that noise?"

"I hear nothing," said the rich man.

"Listen," she said, holding up her forefinger.

The men listened, and a great stillness fell upon the company. Each man, seeing that the rich man listened, listened also, and the opera singer sat with his piano at his fingers, and his fingers silent upon the keys.

"I do hear a noise," said the rich man at length. "A noise as of distant thunder. It is coming nearer and nearer. What can it be?"

They all heard it now, and each seemed ready to start to his feet as he listened. Yet all sat perfectly still. The noise came rapidly nearer.

"What can it be?" said the rich man again.

Tiffany and the Lowlifes

"I think it must be another storm coming over the city," said Mister Marshall.

Then Jonny, who at the first word of the rich man had slipped from his seat, and laid his ear to the floor, rose up quickly, and approaching the rich man said, speaking very fast:

"Please, Sir, I think I know what it is. I have no time to explain, for that might make it too late for some of us. Will you please give orders that everybody leave the house as quickly as possible and get up the hill?"

The rich man, who was one of the wisest men in the country, knew well there was a time when things must be done and questions left till afterwards. He had faith in Jonny, and rose instantly, with Tiffany in his arms.

"Every man and woman follow me," he said, and strode out into the darkness.

Before he had reached the gate the noise had grown to a great thundering roar, and the ground trembled beneath their feet, and before the last of them had crossed the court, out after them from the Great Hall door came a huge rush of turgid water, and almost swept them away. But they got safe out of the gate and up the hill, while the torrent went roaring down the road into the valley beneath.

Jonny had left the rich man and the little rich girl to look after his mother, whom he and his father, one on each side, caught up when the stream overtook them and carried safe and dry.

When the rich man had gotten out of the way of the water, a little up the hill, he stood with the little rich girl in his arms, looking back with amazement on the issuing torrent, which glimmered fierce and foamy through the night. There Jonny rejoined them.

"Now, Jonny," said the rich man, "what does it mean? Is this what you expected?"

"In a way, Sir," said Jonny; and proceeded to tell him about the scheme of the lowlifes, who had resolved, if they should fail in

161

carrying off the rich man's daughter, to flood the underworld of the city. The lowlifes had, in pursuance of their design, let loose all the underground reservoirs and streams, expecting the water to run down into the PG&E and BART tunnels and garages, which were for the most part lower than their parts of the underworld, for they had, as they supposed, not knowing of the solid wall close behind, broken a passage through into it. But the readiest outlet the water could find had turned out to be the tunnel they had made to the rich man's house, the possibility of which catastrophe had not occurred to the young carwasher until he had laid his ear to the floor of the hall.

What was then to be done? The house appeared in danger of falling, and every moment the torrent was increasing.

"We must set out at once!" said the rich man. "But how to get at the cars?"

"Shall I see if we can manage that?" said Jonny.

"Do," said the rich man.

Jonny gathered the bodyguards, and took them over the garden wall, and so to the garage. They found the cars; the water was rising fast around them, and it was quite time they were taken out. But there was no way to get them out, except by driving them through the stream, which was now pouring from the lower windows as well as the door. As one car was quite enough for any man to manage through such a torrent, Jonny got in the king's white limousine and, leading the way, brought them all in safety to the rising street.

"Look, look, Jonny!" cried Tiffany, the moment that, having slowed to a stop, he got out in front of the rich man.

Jonny did look, and saw, high in the air, somewhere about the top of the rich man's house, a great globe of light, shining like the purest silver.

"Oh!" he cried in some consternation, "That is your grandmother's lamp! We must get her out. I will go and find her. The house may fall, you know.

Tiffany and the Lowlifes

"My grandmother is in no danger," said Tiffany, smiling.

"Here, Jonny, take Tiffany while I get in my car," said the rich man.

Jonny took the little rich girl again, and both turned their eyes to the globe of light. The same moment there shot from it a white bird, which descending with outstretched wings, made one circle round the rich man and Jonny and Tiffany, and then glided up again. The light and the pigeon vanished together.

"Now, Jonny," said the little rich girl, as he lifted her to her father's arms, "you see my grandmother knows all about it, and isn't frightened. I believe she could walk through that water and it wouldn't wet her a bit."

"But, my child," said the rich man, "you will be cold if you haven't something more on. Run, Jonny, my boy and fetch anything you can lay your hands on, to keep Tiffany warm. We have a long drive before us."

Jonny was gone in a moment, and soon returned with a great rich fur, and the news that dead lowlifes were tossing about in the current through the house. They had been caught in their own snare; instead of the people of San Francisco's daylight world having their way of life ruined, the lowlifes had flooded their own country, whence they were now swept up from, drowned. Tiffany shuddered, but the rich man held her close to his chest. Then he turned to Mister Marshall, and said:

"Bring Jonny's father and mother here."

"I wish," said the rich man, when they stood before him, "to take your son with me. He shall be given the best education money and care can give, and will be granted a position in one of my companies when the time is right."

Earl Mo and his wife, overcome, only murmured almost inaudible thanks. But Jonny spoke aloud.

"Please, Sir," he said, "I cannot leave my father and mother."

"That's right, Jonny!" cried the little rich girl. "I wouldn't if I was you."

The rich man looked at the little rich girl and then at Jonny with a glow of satisfaction on his countenance.

"I too think you are right, Jonny," he said, "And I will not ask you again. But I shall have a chance of doing something for you some time."

"Helping you has been my pleasure," said Jonny.

"But, Jonny," said his mother, "why shouldn't you go with the rich man? We can get on very well without you."

"But I can't get on very well without you," said Jonny. "The rich man is very kind, but I could not be half the use to him that I am to you. Please, Sir, if you wouldn't mind giving my mother a new coat! I should have bought her one long ago, but for the lowlifes."

"As soon as we get back to the office," said the rich man, "Tiffany and I will search out the best coat to be found, and send it by private messenger."

"Yes, that we will, Jonny!" said the little rich girl. "And next summer we'll come back and see you wear it, Mrs. Mo," she added. "Can't we, Papa?"

"Yes, my love; I hope so," said the rich man.

Then turning to the other workers around, he said:

"Will you do the best you can for my servants tonight? I hope they will be able to return to the house tomorrow."

The garage workers with one voice promised their hospitality.

Then the rich man commanded his servants to mind whatever Jonny should say to them, and after shaking hands with him and his father and mother, the rich man and the little rich girl and all their company rode away down the side of the new stream, which had already devoured half the road, into the starry night.

Chapter 32

All the rest went into the city, and separated in groups to the homes of the garage workers. Jonny and his father and mother took Nursie with them. And the whole way a light, of which all but Nursie understood the origin, shone upon their path. But when they looked round they could see nothing of the silvery globe.

For days and days the water continued to rush from the doors and windows of the rich man's house, and a few lowlifes' bodies were swept out into the road.

Jonny saw that something must be done. He spoke to his father and the rest of the workers, and they at once proceeded to make another outlet for the waters. By setting all hands to the work, tunneling here and building there they soon succeeded; and having also made a little tunnel to drain the water away from under the rich man's house, they were soon able to get into the wine cellar, where they found a multitude of dead lowlifes...among the rest the queen, with the skin-sock gone, and the Army boot fast to her ankle...for the water had swept away the barricade which prevented the bodyguards from following the lowlifes, and had greatly widened the passage. They built it securely up, and then went back to their labours in the garage.

A good many of the lowlifes with their creatures escaped from the inundation out upon the streets of the city. But most of them soon left that part of the country, and most of those who remained grew milder in character, and indeed became very much like street people in every major city. Their skulls became softer as well as their hearts, and their feet grew harder, and by degrees they became friendly with the inhabitants of the city and even with the garage and PG&E workers. But the latter were merciless to any of the lowlifes' creatures that came in their way, until at length they all but disappeared.

And never fear, there is much more to tell of the history of Tiffany and Jonny; but that must be kept for another volume.